G000045321

Mam

'A rare and poignant insight into a typical day for a person caring at home for a loved one with advancing dementia. This is essential reading for family carers everywhere and would also make an excellent addition to the curriculum for professional carer training.'
Mary Hickey, Alzheimer Society of Ireland

'Kieran allows us the privilege of entering the very real world of a carer in such a thoughtful presentation of the minutiae (sometimes uncomfortable) that carers contend with on a given day. The details are carefully intermingled with absorbing reflections on two life stories that hold the reader's attention. It is a beautiful book that gives a lovely insight into caring for and caring about a loved one.'
Prof. Joe Carthy, Director of UCD in the Community

'Insightful, eloquent and compassionate narrative about the relationship between a son caring for his mother with dementia. It touches on core family values, love, loyalty and commitment. A deeply rewarding book.'
Deirdre Hayes, family therapist, lecturer in Masters in Systemic Psychotherapy, PPDI co-ordinator and clinical supervisor, UCD School of Medicine

'Kieran's book is written with great tenderness and sensitivity. It respects and returns the care to him through his life. This book will evoke many memories for the reader.'
Dr Bernadette Mangan, member of the Royal College of Psychiatrists, retired psychiatrist and board member of St John of God Hospital and St Joseph's Dementia Care at Shankill

'What an expression of the unconditional love a son has for his mam. Kieran's expression of his love is going through a time most sons wouldn't envisage for themselves, but he is lucky as he remembers all aspects of his mam and what makes her, her. Honouring his mam through his memories of her life eases his burden of care, but, importantly, it reminds us all that behind the fragility and loss of dementia the person is still there. Thank you, Kieran, for beautifully capturing that even when physical ability, cognition, recognition, and expression is taken away by dementia, love remains.'

Siobhan Grant, St John of God Dementia Care at St Joseph's Shankill, Ireland's largest dementia-specific home

'Kieran Coote has written an extraordinary book describing a family's experience of dementia through the device of a single day. When his mother is diagnosed, Kieran is told he has "the right stuff" to manage, but a wise man also tells him: "You cannot do it from the outside, Kieran. You will have to go into your Mam's world."

Kieran writes incredibly movingly of his daily caring routine. In the tiny details he encompasses whole worlds: the strangeness of becoming a parent to your parent; the depths of patience and resilience needed to counter the daily frustrations; the brutal assaults of anticipatory grief, that grief for a loved one who is still alive but who also has somehow left you behind.

He never doubts why he continues on when at his core he longs to give up, describing how the basic instinct of nourishing loved ones "is deeply built into our DNA". At the worst times, he remembers how, as a young man at his lowest, he "went home again, to my centre, to Mam".

Kieran and his mam make their way through a day that also embraces a life. Kieran has 'walked the walk', and anyone on the same path will find a comforting companion in this book.

Máire O'Dwyer, author of *At the Coalface: A Family Guide to Caring for Older People in Ireland*

Mam an' Me

Living a Lifetime in a Day

Kieran J. Coote

Published by
Red Stripe Press
Upper Floor, Unit B3
Hume Centre
Hume Avenue
Park West Industrial Estate
Dublin 12
Ireland

email: info@redstripepress.com
www.redstripepress.com

© Kieran Coote, 2024

Paperback ISBN 978-1-78605-225-4
ePub ISBN 978-1-78605-226-1

This book is not intended as a clinical guide to dementia or as a substitute for professional advice. The reader should always consult a relevant professional when required. If the reader is emotionally impacted by the story or has any health concerns they should seek professional guidance through their GP.

The publisher has made every effort to contact all copyright holders but if any have been overlooked, they will be pleased to make any necessary arrangements.

A catalogue record for this book is available from the British Library. All rights reserved. No part of this publication may be reproduced, stored in a retrieval system or transmitted in any form or by any means, electronic, mechanical, photocopying, recording or otherwise, without the prior, written permission of the publisher.

This book is sold subject to the condition that it shall not, by way of trade or otherwise, be lent, resold, hired out, or otherwise circulated without the publisher's prior consent in any form of binding or cover other than that in which it is published and without a similar condition including this condition being imposed on the subsequent purchaser.

Printed in Dublin by SPRINTprint Ltd

To all those who have cared, are caring for and will care in the future for their loved ones.

Patricia, aged 16

CONTENTS

FOREWORD

In this deeply touching story, we accompany author Kieran
Coote and his mother, Patricia, as Kieran takes on the role of
her primary carer, as she loses her independence to dementia.

This book is their story. It is a powerful account of their
intertwined lives; of filial gratitude; of maternal devotion; and
of a mother and son 'bound together on a path of duty, choice
and love'. As Kieran brings us, Joycean-like, through a day as
a carer, interspersed with his vivid recollections of childhood
and adolescence, we come to know and admire them both.
We hear his mother's story; the intensity of her love for her
sons; her presence in their lives; her stoicism in the face of
personal loss; the death of her baby son, Alan; the sadness in
her marriage and its ending; and later the demise of family
members from dementia and from motor neurone disease.
Finally, we witness how Patricia retains her gentle soul despite
the erosion of her ability to look after herself, calmed by her
son's compassionate care for her in all the ways her dementia
requires. This is one of the features that makes this book
special, because it is more than a single story of care but of the
dyadic relationship that caring involves and how to cope 'not
from the outside' but by mentally and emotionally entering
into the world of the person within.

Psychologically, dementia is one of our most feared conditions as 'dementia worry' sweeps across the Western world's aging demographic amid the apparent inverse capacity of health care systems to cope. Caring for parents has become a major issue along a continuum that begins with more visits home; help with household tasks, cleaning, laundry, shopping, meals; accompanying parents to medical appointments; and monitoring medications until, in the case of dementia, parental capacities decrease while the need for family support increases exponentially. Not all families are ready for this. Not all family members are equally able or resourced to assist, depending on the circumstances in their own lives, their proximity to the parental home, their lifecycle stage, whether they have other care demands with children, their personal finances, and their prior relationship with the parent in need.

While research examines dementia it in all its dimensions and differentials, initial behavioural changes can be invisible, then unpredictable, confusing and difficult to track. We see Kieran's realisation that the initial occasional quirks in his mother's active, gregarious, independent life are not age-related aberrant incidents but an accumulation of worrying symptoms of decline.

These gradational behavioural changes in dementia can become alarming for families. Appointments may be forgotten, arrangements misunderstood, there may be disorientation in time and space. Days may meld into each other. Events of thirty years ago may be remembered as if they were yesterday and the events of yesterday beyond recall. There may be difficulty doing familiar tasks, which can reach dangerous levels with pots left on hobs, hall doors open or unlocked, objects 'tidied' into strange places and judgement may be impaired.

Kieran gives a fine example of this when his mother brought home a stranger she met to lend him money, and his description of her lack of insight around driving show clearly how behavioural change can be very distressing for everybody. 'Everyday forgetting' becomes forgetting every day or not even discerning that anything untoward has happened. When the reality of the decline becomes undeniable life is altered unutterably for everyone.

There follows Kieran's moving account of his search for information, and for assessment, diagnosis and direction. We see him mine deeply into his resilience. We see his resolution to keep going when the demands of his role as carer overwhelm him and his determination to mind his mother in her own home despite all that lies ahead.

The minding involved is intensive. There is no time off. Psychologically, the reality of progressive dementia is incremental loss and the daily grief of witnessing the erasure of someone we love. There are piercing moments as Kieran's story progresses when mother and son seem equally stunned by the situation in which they find themselves; when she looks with poor recognition at this 'stranger' and he looks back into vacant eyes. When he sees her fragile hands; the stopped watch upon her wrist; the lithe, ethereal frame; the vanishing mother who had always been his surety, his security, his sanctuary and home. Her dementia silences her. Her words are few, often echolalic or minimal responses to Kieran's gentle words to her. She follows instructions slowly, her movements unsteady, counted in steps in a mother–son dance of duty and despair.

And as a backdrop to the silence, our ears are filled with the strains of Puccini's 'Sono andati', the second movement of

Beethoven's fifth piano concerto, and the adagio from Joaquín Rodrigo's 'Concierto de Aranjuez' so beautifully accompanying Kieran's narrative of their lives.

Kieran's account is not only poetic and empathic, but his book invites us to abandon gender stereotypes and to recognise the exquisite, gentle depth of men's practical capacity to be carers too. He shows their sensitivity, their inner pain (so often hidden and unspoken) and their wish to accompany parents through their declining years. We also see the humour in situations as some of Kieran's stories move us from tears to laughter and back again. Additionally, the psychological guidance in relation to communicating with someone suffering from dementia emphasises the importance of not asking direct questions, not contradicting, listening carefully, respecting unreservedly, recognising that the person with dementia is the expert on the experience of dementia and the importance of seeking cues to their inner world. Kieran, with natural attunement to his mother's needs, demonstrates all of the above.

From a clinical perspective, Kieran shows that there is not one patient in his story – there are two. He and his mother have equal if different needs. In a caring society attention to carers is crucial to maintaining their capacity to cope. Carers' lives, their hopes, their independence and their worlds are also compromised by dementia because it is hard to give oneself daily to the minutest needs of another and in doing so to suspend the self. There is the investment of time and attention, the moments when frustration at the relentless demands is overwhelming, and the seeming lack of recognition of two lives in decline – that of carer and cared for. Reality is suspended for both in a bubble of isolation, with the endpoint being grief and guilt at the relief that the end may bring.

These glimpses in Kieran's story show the isolation and the loneliness of his role. Kieran decided not to seek outside help in caring for his mother, and his resilience as a carer shines throughout the book. But additional support for Patricia's care would have been forthcoming from the HSE, had Kieran reached out. Indeed, Kieran's narrative also shows the importance of the many wonderful services and supports available in Ireland, including the physical help that the HSE provides, the advice and insights of the family GP, and the excellent voluntary organisations such as Care Alliance Ireland, Family Carers Ireland, the Palliative Hub and the Alzheimer Society of Ireland.

Kieran's book is filled with pathos, grace, practicality and purpose, with privileged access to the detail and depths of the caring experience. His story has universal application in its call to see behind dementia to the person who resides within. While responses to being cared for may not be made, while gratitude may not be expressed, while understanding of the toll on the carer may not be recognised, Kieran's words leave us in no doubt that behind the dark glass of dementia lies a soul that sees, feels, hears, intuits, loves and continues in a different but nonetheless beauteous relationship with those who care.

Dr Marie Murray,
Clinical psychologist and adjunct professor, School of Psychology,
UCD

PREFACE

I have had a busy life, at times an interesting one. Some days I wonder how I made it this far more or less in one piece. I have had a few edges knocked off me here and there, mostly through my own actions. I understand more clearly now that my life, up to now, has been a series of ups and downs. When I look back over my shoulder, I see the outline of the hills and valleys of my past and realise that little of the important detail remains. The curve and line of the rhythm of my life is steep in places, sharper, and in other places broader and more lenient. I think any one of us, after travelling enough distance, after living enough of this life, could and would say the same.

Something that does make a difference, that makes each soul's journey unique, is the people we meet and cross paths with. Some of these paths are pre-ordained and set a tempo, grading the quality of the early light we will travel with. Our parents, siblings, aunts and uncles, our cousins. Other paths we choose to cross, or to run parallel with for a time. Paths of learning, paths of personal growth, paths of love and intimate relationship. Some paths cross ours because they need to. Work and career paths, sport, and the pathways of ambition. Some paths we are unlucky to cross: paths of violence; paths of abuse, physical, mental, or self. Again, looking back, all the pathways that have touched my life have added or taken away, at one time or another, from my own undulation.

I can say now, openly and clearly, that at this moment I am exactly where I am meant to be. All my different paths and pathways have led, very simply, to now. It is nobody's fault but mine, as the song says. I am responsible for me. Nobody was there all the time to make or influence the central pathway of my life. I alone have that responsibility and I would not like to have it any other way.

I say this now to give you a starting point for our book, *Mam an' Me*. Our paths, Mam's and mine, have run together for over fifty years, sometimes side by side, sometimes crossing over. We have had many years where we lost sight of each other altogether. In recent years we have run very close and closer still. And now, in these last years, our paths, and our lives, have become bound together. Again I say, I am exactly where I am meant to be. For Mam, though, the nature of her illness has taken away some of her choice. I am certain that she would not wish it to be so for either of us.

This book is a record for you, in the simplest way, of what a day is like for two people bound by love and the terrible illness of Alzheimer's/dementia. The frustration and the enlightenment that go hand in hand on any given day. The level of care that is required when your good intentions need to be turned into good actions. The gratitude for all the people close and not so close who come forward to help us and assist in so many ways.

I know that we are not the first or only people bound together on this path of duty, choice and love. I write now for all those who have gone before us on this journey, and for the wisdom and kindness they have imparted to Mam and me along the way. I write also in solidarity with all the fellow souls who find themselves, in this moment, bound on a similar pathway. And finally, I record our experience for any fellow travellers who may one day find themselves in a comparable situation, and are filled with questions, uncertainties, and a myriad of not so clear choices.

For as long as I can remember the radio was always on in our house, 24 hours a day. Mam grew up in a busy house with lots of brothers and sisters, lots of noise and activity. She never liked to come home to a quiet house. 'A quiet house is an empty house,' and Mam did not like the silence. She was the youngest of her siblings and the silence reminds her too much of those who have gone before her. I have included in this book, among the words, some of the music that we have learned to love and share, mostly from the deep and broad vaults of the wonderful Lyric FM.

Finally, I say to everyone, whoever you are, wherever you find yourself, that it is possible to live a lifetime in a day.

Kieran

1.

MORNING

It is Monday, the nineteenth day of July, and forecast to be the hottest day of the year so far. At the broad end of our wedge-shaped green two small stands of forty-foot trees sway gently in the mildest of sea breezes. Above, the cerulean sky spreads to infinity, hazy in the shimmer of the morning sun. My aged red car pants idly on the new concrete drive, enclosed sideways by the large box hedge and our neighbour's fence.

Our front door stands open wide and the warm breeze works its way through the hall and downstairs rooms. From the radio upstairs the opening notes of Puccini's 'Sono andati' cascade lightly down the staircase:

Have they gone? I pretended to be asleep because I wanted to be alone with you.

I climb the stairs again with a familiar weary heaviness, drawn by the music, the voice of soprano Mirella Freni and my strong sense of duty.

The door to Mam's bedroom is open.

1

I've so many things to tell you ... or rather only one.

I step lightly under the lintel and look round the door to my mother's bed and Mam, propped up with pillows, in a vest and covered with the lightest green blanket.

But that one huge as the ocean, as deep and infinite as the sea.

She sleeps, or dozes, her head turned slightly towards me. Her face has the aged grey pallor of her illness and at her slightly open mouth a small trickle of moisture glistens. If not for the faint rise and fall of the coverlet from her shallow breathing, I could believe that Mam has died, is dead. A part of me wishes that today, it was so. For her mostly and, a little guiltily, for me too.

You are my love and my whole life.

I drum my fingers lightly on the door and enter, shrugging away the unwanted heaviness I feel.

'Good morning, Mam, good morning.' I move across the room and open the curtain a little.

'Good morning, love, did you have a good sleep?'

Her eyes open slowly as I lean over her and lightly brush the hair back from her forehead, dabbing her mouth with a paper tissue.

'Will I put the kettle on?'

'Good morning, good morning,' she repeats. 'Put the kettle on, put the kettle on' she whispers, and closes her eyes again. Our dog Scamp, Mam's favourite son, I believe, yawns from his place at the foot of the bed and stretches. He is as familiar with the routine as I am.

It was dark, and you couldn't see me blushing.
What a frozen little hand, let me warm it for you ...
It was dark and you took my hand ...

Downstairs again, kettle on and boiling, a slice of brown bread toasting; familiar morning sounds and smells. I turn up the radio and open the back door wide.

My heaviness returns from its chamber, somewhere just below my centre. Up and through my heart, filling my limbs and head. It is a sadness I know. It can be triggered and well up at any time, a little more frequently nowadays. It seems like a deep pool full to my emotional brim. One more sad thought, one more strong emotion and it threatens to overflow from my eyes and overwhelm me. I take a deep breath and choke it down. There will be time enough for it somewhere in the days ahead, I say to myself, but not now.

I continue with the morning routine, taking the milk, marmalade and margarine from the fridge in the corner.

The house continues to waken and through the upstairs floorboards I hear my daughters stirring. Doors open and close and the toilet flushes. Music comes on low in the girls' room. Certainly not Puccini!

Tea and toast in hand, I retrace my steps upstairs, navigating past the stairlift. I place the cup and side plate on the bedside dresser to cool down a little.

'Morning, Mam,' a little louder than before. 'There's a nice cup of tea here for you now.'

This time Mam's eyes open wider, brighter. A little of her old self briefly comes to the surface.

'A nice cup of tea,' she says softly.

I pull back her blanket and in much-practised moves manage to slowly turn and pull her into a sitting position on the edge of her bed. Her left knee is swollen again, the rest of her legs thin and pale. I hold her soft, fragile hands as she gathers herself.

'We're going to stand up now, Mam, when you're ready. Okay, one, two, three.'

I lean back, standing, pulling Mam towards me, and she slowly rises. Her legs straighten as much as they can and with her back bent and arms out, she takes a first small tentative step.

'Nice and easy now, Mam, one small step at a time,' I say encouragingly, 'No rush.'

We make it the twenty paces to the bathroom on the upstairs landing.

'Now hold on to the handrail with both hands and I'll help you with your pants.'

I ease down her safety pants and pyjamas to her knees and, holding her waist, I turn her slowly, so she hovers above the loo.

'Now sit down there for a second.'

She does, creaking in knees and hips.

I kneel in front of her and remove the pyjamas and pants.

At eye level our gaze meets. Mam's eyes narrow. I wonder what is going through her mind right now. Sometimes she looks as if she does not understand how we got here. What am I doing, her son, in the bathroom while she is going to the loo? Sometimes there is a look of fear. Other times she looks at me like I am a stranger. I shift my gaze and pretend not to notice her confusion.

I use soothing tones when I speak with her, trying to let her know that everything is okay. I try to say the same things, at the same time, in the same way. It has a calming effect. Mam may not remember or understand the words I use but responds to the rhythm of my voice.

'I'll get you a fresh pair; I'll be back in a flash.'

'Get a fresh pair, get a fresh pair', follows me to the landing, where all her toilet things are stored.

I give her a moment and again the heaviness rises. A memory this time, a picture in black and white, an old one, without sound. It is my first day going to school aged four or five. Mam is unwell and our neighbour Kay O'Neill is standing at our front door waiting to bring me. Before I walk down our garden path I turn and look up at Mam. I can see her beautiful face as clearly as if it were yesterday. She was 35 years old then.

My eyes fill, and inside, in my chamber, I hear another drop fall and echo across the taut dark surface of my pool. *Not yet, no, not yet,* I echo back.

'I'll be back in a flash, I'll be back in a flash', from behind the closed bathroom door brings me back to the moment again. I swallow hard and tell myself to cop on.

'Are you finished, love, are you happy enough?' I ask two or three times, as Mam balances on the edge of the loo.

'Yes, I'm happy enough,' she replies eventually. I pull a long piece from the toilet roll and fold it for her to use. 'We're going to stand up now, dear,' I say as I take her offered hands. 'One, two, three.' I hold firm and now we are standing.

'Let's give our hands a rinse,' I say, edging and turning her towards the sink. She holds on to the sink as I run the water and pour the liquid soap for her. Legs braced, she rubs her hands together and rinses. I check her progress. Sometimes she forgets to rinse a hand. I half turn her again, towards the dry hand towel hanging on the door of the converted shower. I wait patiently as she dries her hands and meticulously replaces the towel, smoothing out any creases.

'Now let's put on this fresh pair,' I say, kneeling again.

'Lift your foot, yes, that's it, and the other foot, please, that's great Mam.' I pull up the fresh pair of pants, adjusting the waistband, making sure they are sitting snugly against her skin. We repeat the manoeuvre with her pyjama bottoms.

We hold hands again and slowly retrace our twenty steps, me walking backwards, to the bedroom.

'Are you ready for a nice cup of tea?' I ask.

There is no reply. Mam is focusing all her concentration on taking each one of her twenty small steps.

Back in her room again we pirouette, exchanging sides, and Mam sits down on the edge of her bed. She sees the tea and toast waiting on the bedside dresser.

'Oh, a nice cup of tea,' she coos as she lifts the mug to her lips and slurps softly.

The son and boy inside me smiles; I am pleased that she is pleased. I am happy that for this one moment, one action, she seems like her old self again.

I sit down beside her on the edge of the bed and point to the toast on the plate next to her cup. 'There's a slice of toast there for you too, with marmalade.'

She picks up a slice and examines it before taking a small bite, then another sip of tea.

We sit there, side by side, for the next few minutes. I remind and encourage her to eat and drink. Mam follows my lead and occasionally looks at me from under her eyebrows. It is that questioning look again: 'What are you doing here, sitting on my bed?' I wait until Mam is almost finished. From experience I know that if I don't wait and take the time for her to drink and eat, she will forget the tea after the first sip, ignore it, and slip back into bed.

I am like the parent now doing the parent things. Poor Mam is slipping back towards infancy, a little more each week. I am afraid of what might come after that. Will I be able to manage? Will I be able to keep her here with me at home? Will Mam and the essence of her become totally lost to her illness?

The radio again, the silver set on Mam's bedside locker. It is on 24 hours a day, tuned to Lyric FM. Mam always had the radio on in the house. Two radios, in fact: one in the kitchen and one, as now, in her bedroom. She was born and raised in this house with her three brothers and four sisters. The house was always active and full of sound. She told me many years ago that without the radio playing in the background the place was too quiet for her. There were too many memories in the silence. Sometimes now I have the sound turned down, but, superstitiously, I don't turn the radio off, ever.

It is the light touch of Marty Whelan at this hour of the morning, Mam's favourite – when she remembered such things. Doris Day's amazing clear voice fills the air, singing 'Close Your Eyes', accompanied by double bass and piano.

I stand up. Mam's tea is finished and more than half her toast.

'I'll pop you back into bed for a bit, Mam', I say. She nods and turns into the bed.

I lift her legs together, swing them slowly into the centre of the bed and pull her coverlet up around her waist. She is propped up again against her three-stack of pillows and slowly, with a last look at the stranger, she closes her eyes again.

I hope Mam dreams of something like dancing, knowing I am always here by her side.

2.

DIAGNOSIS

It was not always like this, of course.

Mam was diagnosed with the early symptoms of dementia in April 2018. There had been many signs during the year and in the previous year. Some very minor, like forgetting people's names, confusing places she had been to and people she had met. 'Everyday forgetting' I called it. I didn't pay too much attention and assumed it was just part of getting older. I have been known to forget the odd thing myself from time to time.

From February 2017 some out of the ordinary incidents began to happen. Mam, though, was quite unaware of the danger or the significance of the incidents. The fact that Mam did not react, in any kind of understanding way, to the incidents added to my concern for her. So much so that I began to keep a journal of some of the things that were happening.

2017

FEBRUARY

I came home during the day and found the front door open and Mam asleep on her chair with her coat on.

Mam set a tea towel on fire in the kitchen. She had left the gas lit on the cooker and put the tea-towel down close by and it had caught fire. The smoke alarm went off and thankfully I was upstairs. I raced down and smothered the fire. The new kitchen counter was scorched and blistered, but Mam was not injured.

MARCH

The front door of the house was open and nobody was home. Mam had gone to the post office.

I came home in the evening and Mam had lit the fire in the front room and piled on briquettes, which were burning fiercely. Mam was in the back room watching telly; she said she had forgotten about the fire.

MAY

My daughter called down to the house in the afternoon and found a gas ring on the cooker fully lit. Mam was watching telly in the back room and said she did not leave any gas ring on. She was confused and said she might have but forgot about doing so.

***

In early June I needed to find out more about what was going on mentally with Mam. I made an appointment with her own doctor of many years, under the ruse of her yearly check-up. I explained a little of what had occurred during the past few months as the doctor checked Mam's blood pressure and weight. She was kind and understanding and gave Mam a mini-memory test or MMSE (mini-mental status examination).

It was a strange experience, the three of us sitting together in the small surgery with eye charts and diagrams of human anatomy on the walls. A full skeleton stood leeringly in the corner and out through the long office window the blue sky framed a single white cloud. Inside again, me trying to explain to the doctor what was going on with Mam, sotto voce, nodding and winking, aware that Mam is sitting beside me and watching everything. The doctor listening and trying to get the gist of what I'm saying and Mam, fidgeting in her chair, aware that something is not right, but not sure what or why.

During the MMSE, the doctor asked Mam a series of simple questions designed to test the range of her everyday mental skills. Questions like, what month is it? Write down your own name. Identify common items. Simple things like that.

As the doctor went through the questions, I looked sideways at Mam and she was giving me the eyes, as if to say, 'Why she is asking me these silly and childish questions?'

I kept patting Mam's hand, sensing her unease and discomfort with the questions and the situation.

The maximum MMSE score is 30 points. A score of 20 to 24 suggests mild dementia, 13–20 moderate dementia, and less than 12 severe dementia. On average, the MMSE score of a person with Alzheimer's declines about two to four points each year.

Mam scored 25, which was inconclusive as far as the test was concerned.

The doctor spoke about diet and an exercise routine for Mam. I was not really listening, though. Deep down inside me I felt the beginnings of a fear. A fear based on experience and familiarity with this illness. Mam's sisters Pauline and Betty and her brother Frank had all contracted and died from complications that go hand-in-hand with dementia. I had taken Mam to visit them many times over the years and saw at each visit the decline and inevitability of their illness.

The doctor finished by suggesting that I might keep a journal of some kind to record things. I was ahead of her there, for once. We thanked her and left, Mam asking too loudly what that was all about.

***

JULY

I came home one evening to find the gas fully lit in the kitchen and the fire in the front room blazing away again. Mam was asleep in her chair by the fire, hot and sweating. When I calmed the fire down Mam explained that she had lit a bit of newspaper from the gas to light the fire and forgot to switch off the gas ring.

OCTOBER

The gas fire in the back room was turned on to its full three bars by Mam with the windows and door closed. I came home and Mam was asleep in the chair, the room like a furnace. I woke Mam, who was in a deep sleep and again very hot and sweating. I know that gas fires are dangerous and installed a carbon monoxide alarm in the room.

2. Diagnosis

Mam put a chicken in the oven with the plastic tray still underneath it. I arrived home, noticed the acrid smell and dealt with the situation. Mam, even though she was downstairs, was unaware of the awful smell. Thankfully, the chicken had been in the oven less than half an hour.

***

You might be thinking, after reading the above, why I didn't lock the kitchen door when I wasn't there or change the lock on the front door or take other precautions like that. But between these incidents Mam was her old self. She was making her own tea and toast each morning, frying a rasher, too, when she wanted one. She tackled the *Irish Times* crossword every day and often almost completed it. Every morning she walked to Mass in Fairview church or took the 123 bus to the Pro Cathedral on Marlborough Street. On Saturday mornings she had her hair done in Peter Mark's on O'Connell Street and then did her shopping in town for whatever bits and pieces she needed.

Mam was also a regular and active member of the Fairview and Marino ladies' club; she had been a member for many years. She frequently went on bus trips with the ladies all over the country and was always one of the first to sign up for a trip. Mam had lots of friends and acquaintances in the area and was always chatting with someone on a corner. In none of these areas of her life was anything untoward noticed – or if it was, I was never made aware of it.

It is such a difficult thing to fathom when you have no practical experience. When do you step in and take control of a situation, and when do you not? I wanted Mam to remain in control and have as much independence as possible. She is my mother, after all. She was always so independent, had always been the one taking care of me. Sometimes you get it wrong, mostly because you do not know any better. I seemed to be always playing catch-up with the situation. I felt like I was trying to help from the outside.

I followed my own intuition and the doctor's advice and carried on with my journal.

2018

JANUARY

I came home from the supermarket late in the morning and Mam had gone out. She had not mentioned earlier that she was going out. She did not answer her mobile, but that is not unusual. I waited an hour and then checked around the local area, café, church, etc. and couldn't find her. A friend of Mam's rang at 1.30 in the afternoon to say she was sitting in the Pro Cathedral with her.

FEBRUARY

Mam arrived home from Mass with a stranger. He promptly left when I challenged him. Mam said they met outside church, and she was going to lend him some money.

MARCH

I came home from the supermarket and Mam was eating an unheated cottage pie taken from the fridge. She was not unwell afterwards, thankfully.

Mam had lit a huge fire in the front room, had not put the fire guard in front of the fire and was watching TV in the back room. The gas was still on. Mam had forgotten about the fire.

We had a big argument about Mam refusing to take a shower. Half an hour later she had completely forgotten about the incident.

APRIL

Gas ring left on and oven on. Mam had gone to collect her pension. Unfortunately, she had collected her pension the day before.

Mam got into an argument at her local ladies' club. She insisted she had paid a deposit for a trip or outing. Her best friend, Chrissy, was sure Mam had not paid the deposit yet. This was unheard of from Mam. Mam is such a gentle soul, and this was an incredibly sad day.

I found Mam asleep and chilled in the back garden, on a chair, front and back door open, at about seven in the evening.

***

One more significant incident happened towards the end of April that brought everything together and caused me to completely change my approach to the reality of what was going on. It happened on Wednesday morning, the twenty-fifth. I drove Mam to the Pro Cathedral for eleven o'clock Mass. I parked on Cathedral Street opposite Brannigans pub and walked Mam, arm in arm, up the back steps to the side entrance of the church.

'Are you not coming in?' she asked at the door.

'I'll be in in a minute,' I lied. 'I'll just finish my cigarette.'

She nodded and gave me the mother's eye. She knew she would have to light a candle for me and say a couple of extra Hail Marys for telling lies to her on the church grounds. It was like being twelve years old again, Mam grilling me about what the priest had said in his sermon when I'd been sent to Mass as a kid on my own. Even way back then I was standing outside the church smoking cigarettes.

I went back to the car and switched on the radio. It was a chilly morning with no sign of spring in the air. Twenty-five minutes passed and I thought I would slip in and sit beside her for a minute as the Mass ended. She would like that and maybe it would only cost her one extra Hail Mary. I walked around to the front entrance on Marlborough Street, skirted past the beggars sitting on the front steps and went inside.

I got a complete shock! The church was empty apart from one or two poor souls sitting among the many empty rows of pews. I scanned the rows and the nave a second time, then moved right and worked my way around to the back of the altar. Alarm bells were quietly ringing, and I could feel a cold sweat, and my panic, rising. At the back of the altar is the statue to Our Lady where Mam would often light a candle. She was not there. I quickened my step, completed the circuit of the church and went back out of the front entrance. The whole sweep couldn't have taken me more than two minutes.

I sprang down the steps onto Marlborough Street and looked up and down the road. No sign of her. I'm now trying to think what colour coat she was wearing and cursing myself at the same time for not going into Mass with her. *She's gone back to the car* was my next thought and I made my way up Cathedral Street, jogging now.

No sign of her at the car. Another two minutes have passed. She might be gone for the bus? She might be gone up to O'Connell Street? Would she have walked home by herself? As far as I was aware she wasn't carrying any money. I'm sweating now, and my long coat, heavy jumper, scarf and boots worn against the April chill weren't helping. I took off the scarf and started running back down Cathedral Street. I took a right turn onto Marlborough Street and ran towards the bus stops on Eden Quay, scanning the crowd as I ran, panic rising, cursing myself to myself. I reach the Quays and there is no sign of her. I retrace my steps, still running, all the time registering my lack of fitness and hearing my heart beating loudly in my ears.

If you are running through the streets in this part of Dublin, and not wearing a jogging outfit, most local people think you are up to no good. I ignored the questioning looks and made it back to Cathedral Street and the car. She wasn't there. Twenty minutes have passed now; I gulp down a couple of deep breaths and jog up onto O'Connell Street. I cross the road into the centre isle and look all around hoping for a glimpse of her little self. As usual O'Connell Street is full of people, buses and cars. No sign of her! I notice Mam's hairdressers opposite, Peter Mark's, and quickly cross the road again and cup my hands to peer through the large plate glass front window. More strange looks from the ladies working inside. I must look a right state, I thought. Mam is not there.

Thirty minutes or more have passed. I tell myself to calm down and try to quiet the dark thoughts running through my head.

I ring my friend and neighbour Des on the off-chance she has got home somehow. Des answers after a couple of rings. *Thank Christ*, I say to myself.

'Des', I say, trying to control my breathing, 'will you go and knock at my house and see, if by any chance, my mam is home. I'm in town, and I've lost her!'

'Yeah, no problem,' he says and walks out into his front garden.

'There she is, Kieran; she's just walking around the corner now.'

'Thank Christ,' I say again, this time aloud, feeling like a terrible hypocrite and promising to light a couple of candles myself the next time I am in the Pro Cathedral.

'Could you bring her into your house and give her a cup of tea, please? I'll be home in a few minutes.'

'No problem. I'll see you soon.'

The relief is hard to describe. I went back to the car, legs like jelly, and sat for five minutes trying to pull myself together. The 'what ifs' would not stop going round and round in my head. I realised now that I would have to do something more to deal with the situation. The fear rose again from deep inside and I felt the full burden of responsibility finally settle on my shoulders.

When I returned home, I parked the car and called into Des's house. Mam was sitting quietly at his kitchen table with a half-drunk mug of tea beside her.

'Where were you?' she said accusingly, before I could open my mouth, her eyes flashing in a rare show of anger. 'I came home and couldn't get into the house. Des brought me in and gave me a nice cup of tea and a biscuit.'

I exchanged looks with Des, wisely bit my tongue, and thought of strangling her!

The poor dear had forgotten I was waiting outside. When Mass ended, she had left by the front entrance and got a bus home, as she always did, using the bus pass in her purse. It was another example of getting the level of care wrong. I realise I am not on the same wavelength as Mam. More will be required from me. Much more.

Before we leave, I have a cigarette and a chat with Des in his back garden. Des is an advanced nurse practitioner at the Mater, a medical man all the way to his fingertips. He is very experienced and level-headed in these matters and says just what I need to hear at this moment.

'You cannot do it from the outside, Kieran. You will have to go into your Mam's world, see things as she sees them. "Wanting to" will not be enough now unless you want to keep repeating the same mistakes. It will be very frustrating and require a lot of patience and understanding from you. You will get there in the end, though; you have the right stuff inside you.'

He was so right on all accounts.

Three days later I brought Mam for another check-up, this time to a geriatric unit. The tests were more comprehensive, including a brain scan. Another mini-mental state examination or MMSE was carried out by the consultant. These assessments are emotionally difficult. It is hard for a son to witness his mother's decline being measured. A huge protectiveness kicks in. While in our hearts we know how caring those who administer these tests are, they do this on a daily basis. For the family, this is not routine. The outcome is crucial. Professionalism can feel impersonal and matter-of-fact, and the results very hard to absorb. Anger wells up with the pain of having to be there in the first place. The memory test was conducted using plastic animals laid out on the desk as an aid to some of the questions. Mam was very uneasy and again I got the eyes – what is this silliness all about? Mam's vulnerability made me want to flee from the place, as if not knowing the outcome would protect Mam.

Mam scored 21 out of 30, a marked decline over the last nine months of four points, about 12 per cent. When I asked about the results of the brain scan, I was told they showed some damage but because there are so many different types of dementia the consultant explained that they could not tell for certain if Mam had Alzheimer's or dementia. Our aloneness hit me and I swore that my Mam would never go through any more tests.

From now on I was taking charge of everything. Later, in a quiet moment at home, as I contemplated the day and what was ahead, I felt the axis of my world shift. I felt myself turning fully into the reality of our situation. Shoulders, hips, feet and, most important, head. I would meet this challenge head on. I would be alright. We would be alright. With enough courage and resolve I would be able to care for Mam, protect her and keep her safe no matter what came towards us, no matter where it came from.

I did not realise to what extent my courage and resolve would be repeatedly tested. But from now on I was going to look at this experience as part of my journey, our journey. I would choose what type of experience it would be. I had control of that at least.

I will arise and go now, and go to Innisfree,
And a small cabin build there, of clay and wattles made;
Nine bean-rows will I have there, a hive for the honey-bee,
And live alone in the bee-loud glade.

W.B. Yeats

3.

BEFORE NOON

I had the dream again just before I woke at dawn. It is a familiar and recurring one. It comes back to me now, in pieces, in pictures, in haphazard video.

In the dream, I am lying in my bedroom just waking from a deep sleep. It is the afternoon. I had gone to my room for something obscure, briefly let my eyes close and slept. I am disoriented now as I wake and the sunlight coming through the closed curtains is too bright. I blink once, twice, close my eyes tightly then open them again. Now I am standing at the foot of Mam's bed. All the furniture in her bedroom is over-sized. I feel small and childlike, but I am aware that I am not a child. Mam is sitting up in the bed reading a magazine or folded newspaper. She stops reading and lowers the paper. She looks at me with bright eyes, a clear face and with her warm smile. I see no sign of her illness and she looks twenty years younger.

'Good morning, Kieran,' she says. Her voice is calm, strong, normal.

The relief I feel is overwhelming. It floods through me from the top of my head down through my body and limbs all the way to my feet and spills onto the floor.

Mam's okay! Her illness, everything else, was just a dream.

Then the image and feeling, mist-like, dissipate and I am lying alone in the darkness listening to my heart beat.

When I woke this morning, this pictorial incantation lay heavily across my body and across my mind. Before I opened my eyes, I knew it was just that wistful dream again. In my ear I could hear Carl Jung whispering about the important messages from the subconscious waiting to be found in your dreams. Alone then with the sound of my heart, I knew the dream would not change the shape of my day or my days ahead.

It all fades away again now, as I finish my coffee, sitting beneath the lean-to I built a few years ago in my back garden.

The sun has climbed higher in the sky and its heat and light have bleached the bright colours from the scene. The towering box hedge that screens the back from the houses behind is in full flower and fills the light summer breeze with a honeyed fragrance. The drone of the many happy bees suckling there adds a contented hum to the air. It is close to noon and the silver bell of duty calls.

Again, I mount the stairs. Drumming my fingers lightly on the open door, I enter Mam's room. She is awake now, thumbing through the pages of Tony's book for the umpteenth time.

Tony's book usually rests on the white high-backed chair on the far side of her bed. It has been almost two years, but Mam still looks for it each day and likes to have it on the bed beside her. Lately, though, it is the photographs inside she mostly looks at, or she reads the title aloud. '*Live While You Can*, by Father Tony Coote' she says and looks at me blankly.

I used to sit on the bed beside her and try explaining to her in the simplest terms, 'That was your son Tony, Mam, your eldest, he wrote that book. He got a bad disease and died. He is in heaven now with Alan and your brothers and sisters and your mam.'

I never knew if what I said registered with Mam, and, if it did, where? There was never any sign of recognition on her face. She would look at me and hold my gaze for a moment, then lower her eyes and turn a few pages, forgetting me and what I had said.

I felt explaining it to her was upsetting her somehow, somewhere deep inside, where an untouched, unaffected part of her still resided. It upsets me a lot too. They were so close, so strongly connected. *How far things have come*, I thought, *how far they have gone.*

I don't say anything or respond any more. I don't interrupt whatever cycle she is having with these thoughts and actions. I am outside it now; I am unable to understand what she is going through.

I walk slowly around the end of Mam's bed and open the curtains halfway. Sunlight floods in.

'Morning, Mam, did you have a nice nap?'

Mam's eyes follow me, inquiringly. Lately, in the first moments of each interaction between us, Mam has become less sure of who I am, a little less week by week. Again, I use the same words and tone of voice, to give her a chance to come to the surface, to come into the moment with me.

'Would you drink a glass of juice?' I ask, and then repeat it, coming towards her and lifting the cup and side plate from earlier off the bedside dresser.

'I would drink a glass of juice,' she finally answers quietly.

'Right so, I'll organise one and I'll be back in a minute.'

I am the parent again, parenting my parent. It is another veiled role that you discover as you turn willingly into the situation. As a parent myself, I see the parallels of my own parenting experience, and this mirrored experience, much more clearly. It lights up in the paths of my memory and I often wonder why I did not notice it so much before.

Understanding now, after trying unsuccessfully to influence the effect of Mam's illness on her mind, I find that I can have an influence where her bodily-wellbeing is concerned. Like all parents, and it starts from the first day, you become preoccupied with feeding and nourishing your children. It begins with the feeding every two hours when they are newborn. Then the bottles get bigger and the time between the feeding gets correspondingly longer. After three or four months they move on to solid food and so it continues. Your whole life starts to revolve around checking your watch to see when it is time to feed them again.

This necessary and absorbing pattern carries on through the young years and into the teens with diminishing levels of parental enthusiasm. Knowing all this, I continue to do it for my four girls. 'Have you had something to eat?'; 'When did you eat last?'; Would you like a sandwich, bowl of soup, an apple …?' You even give them your own dinner sometimes. And, of course, the young adults play the small child card on you, give you the big eyes, nod their heads and say, 'Yes please, Dad.' And you willingly play along, because the basic instinct of nourishing your loved ones is deeply built into our DNA.

This experience stands me in good stead now. Mam is alive, and needs nourishing food every day to give her body the best possible chance of coping with the situation.

Back downstairs in the kitchen, I pause to centre myself and listen attentively to the radio as the all-powerful voice of Pavarotti completes the 'Recondita Armonia' from *Tosca*. Indeed, this world is filled with a mysterious harmony.

On the kitchen counter my two stainless steel sentinels stand ready; my small squat nut grinder, and his taller, prouder companion, a Tefal blender. They are the third set of stalwarts; their predecessors became worn out over time and were retired. They remind me some mornings of the candle and clock from Disney's *Sleeping Beauty*. If they could talk, I am sure they would ask for the day off! *I know the feeling*, I say to myself.

Each morning, as part of this feeding and nourishing, I make Mam a fruit smoothie and blend a bowl of mixed nuts and seeds. These were the first foods of our ancient hunter-gatherer ancestors and work just as well today as part of Mam's diet. I have tried many different options to get the right balance of flavour, nutrition, simplicity and edibility into this meal. The Mam of old would never have eaten such things. An apple or an orange would be her limit, or a banana in a sandwich when she had a mind to.

In fact, she was an awful woman for giving us kids a banana sandwich for our school lunch back in the day. Whatever the sandwiches looked like when she made them and wrapped them in brown greaseproof paper (this was in the age before clingfilm), they were unrecognisable three hours later when you attempted to eat them in the lunch break. They were a bit like the fast-food ads on the TV nowadays, the well stacked and perfectly made burgers compared to the real thing, all squashed and thrown together, when you open your little foam box. A lot of the boys in my first years in Joey's (St Joseph's CBS, Fairview) had mothers with the same idea and you couldn't move in the yard some days without slipping on one of those discarded sandwiches.

I smile thinking of this now as I assemble the ingredients for the smoothie. This role reversal has some positive sides to it too. One soft banana is always first into the blender!

This morning I also add a Conference pear, a handful of blueberries, a handful of raspberries, a quarter of a fresh juicy pineapple and a ripe fragrant nectarine. Sometimes I use strawberries or soft mangos. I also add four large ice cubes. The smoothie needs to be chilled, or Mam will not enjoy it. I must agree with her there. I add about 150ml each of sugar-free cranberry and pressed apple juice. Put the lid on firmly and turn the knob. The machine whirrs into action, reacting violently with the hardness of the ice cubes for a moment before smoothly carrying on.

Next, I take the seven containers of nuts and mixed seeds from the cupboard overhead. I pour 20–25 cashews into the grinder and add a heaped tablespoon of mixed sunflower, sesame, flax and pumpkin seeds and half a spoon of milled chai seeds. They blend easily together and after half a minute are reduced to a fine crumb. I pour and scrape this first batch into a bowl.

On the chopping board go 10–12 almonds, the same number of walnuts and pecans and three or four Brazil nuts. They are all harder than the rest and need to be chopped into smaller pieces before grinding. I take extra care with my very sharp chopping knife. When sufficiently chopped I give them the same grinder treatment. I add the first batch back in and blend the two to a soft glistening paste. There is something very satisfying watching the mix revolve around waiting for it to reach the right consistency. It is a moment of no-mind and attention; very calming despite the different tones of blending around me. I scrape the contents into the bowl and carefully wash out the grinder .

The mixed nuts and seeds add a rich variety of important fats, minerals and vitamins to Mam's diet. The calorie content they contribute is also important. As a paste, they are very tasty, easy to eat and are digested much faster, putting less strain on Mam's internal organs.

The blender is finished too, and I divide the contents into several glasses, pouring about 300ml for Mam. As always there is a daughter waiting in the wings for a spare glass. 'Yes please, Dad!'

Again, the mix of fruit and juice adds much-needed vitamins, minerals and sugars to Mam's diet. The smoothie is very flavoursome, and I like to imagine it wakens and brightens Mam's palate each morning. The liquid intake is important, too, for helping Mam's bodily functions stay regular and in order.

I pour a large glass for myself as well. That is another positive thing; I get to drink a glass every morning too. I love the cool fruitiness and sense of wellbeing I feel as I drink the first mouthful down. I disassemble the blender and rinse it thoroughly. It cleans very easily if you wash it straightaway and conversely takes ages to clean if you leave it for later.

I add a teaspoon and Mam's morning tablets to the side of the bowl and with practised dexterity carry it and our two glasses of cool pink goodness back up the stairs to her room.

My eldest daughter is hanging round the bedroom door, half inside the room, talking with Mam.

'Good morning, Granny, did you have a good sleep?' she says cheerfully several times.

Mam is looking at her intently.

It's a bit of fun my girls have with their granny, seeing who can get the best response from her. A wave, a smile, a 'Good morning', followed by their name, is considered the best response. A long look from Mam, without comment or action, is considered the worst. Jasmyn gets a wave and then Mam's gaze switches to the smoothie I am carrying. I put the glasses and bowl on the bedside locker and encourage Mam to sit up a bit against her pillows.

'Hoosh up a bit there, Mam' I repeat slowly, a couple of times, varying my tone slightly and wait for her to understand and respond.

Through her eyes I see her mind working and after a moment I see a hint of understanding appear. She moves her arms and carefully pushes herself backwards and upwards. I usually draw the duvet back a little and give her legs a lift. It is important that her back is as straight as possible to help her 'breakfast' go down more easily.

I perch on the side of her bed and offer her a glass.

'Try a drop of that, Mam, it's nice and cool and fruity,' I say, placing the glass carefully in her hand. A slip now would be very messy. I am at full attention, understanding that a little accident now would be my fault. Mam's grip is not what it has been and some mornings she is a little more distant than others.

'Nice and cool and fruity,' she repeats.

She takes the offered glass and drinks successfully. I nearly laugh aloud sometimes at the childish grimace that appears on her face as she takes the first cold, sharp, sweet mouthful. Her palate has awakened!

It's a small sip.

'Isn't that lovely?' I ask mischievously, thinking again of those banana sandwiches.

'Yes,' she lies easily, giving as good as she gets, and hands me back the glass, slipping her hand back under the duvet.

'Now your vitamins,' I add quickly, offering one of her morning tablets and the glass again.

She takes the tablet, places it in her mouth, takes the glass and drinks another mouthful. The grimace is less now, and we repeat the process with the next tablet and the next. Half her smoothie is gone now, and she is starting to enjoy it.

Thankfully, Mam takes very few tablets each day. I know that some of her friends have a huge amount to take every day. It is a constant worry for any carer trying to manage the daily tablet intake. Over the day Mam takes three tablets for her condition and two multivitamins. The tablets do not really work for her any more, if they ever did. She is past the point where they are effective. The vitamins are much the same.

My doctor explained to me, 'If you have a good balanced diet, you really do not need to take any vitamin supplements.' Most doctors, if not all, will tell you the same.

I persist with the tablets, though; since Mam needs to drink something to help swallow them that adds to her overall liquid intake for the day. You cannot imagine how difficult it is sometimes to get Mam to take a drink of water. She makes an even bigger face than when drinking her smoothie, and sometimes, like a child, she will pretend to drink, watching you from beneath her eyebrows as you hover near her.

'Now will you have a little of this?' I ask, holding a half-filled teaspoon of nut paste up to her mouth. She nods, opens her mouth, accepts the offering, and chews cautiously.

'Isn't that nice?' I prompt. 'It's nuts and seeds blended, Mam. Food for the body and food for the brain.'

She nods again and I see a little sign of recognition of the paste and then an acceptance of it. It is an easy eat for her, a warm earthy flavour, neutral in her mouth compared to the cool fruity explosion of the smoothie. The combination works and she accepts another spoonful, chewing thoughtfully.

On the radio, it's Mr Carroll's set, and he's treating us to a string quartet by Boccherini, his Opus 30 No. 6. I turn up the volume and I feel like dancing. The power of the music, its uplifting nature, its light-footed tempo, its timelessness, all fill the room and fill me too. I am also sure that it tinkles and strums somewhere in Mam's musical memory.

We carry on with the spoon-fed nut paste and alternate every few mouthfuls with another sip of smoothie, until both are finished. Mam eats and drinks lightly with a measure of pleasure on her face. It is all I can expect from her during these moments, and it is all that I want too. She is content, stimulated and is being nourished as best as can be.

And I am also being nourished in a separate way. My instinct for what Mam needs at this moment is proved correct. The balance and blend of the meal is a success in terms of diet and flavour and, above all, enjoyment and stimulation for Mam. It is hard to acknowledge the significance of these little moments if you have not been in this position before. You are always asking yourself if you are doing the right thing, at the right time, in the right way. Mam is very silent nowadays and what she is thinking and feeling is a mystery to me most of the time.

There is no 'thank you' any more, or praise or even criticism; she is not in that place now. You need other ways to catch these emotional clues that help to sustain your caring. I have learned that you get back what you give, the essence of karma really. By using good ingredients, preparing them with care, attention and love and taking the time, your time, to allow someone to savour them, you get your reward like the one I am receiving this morning. Though mute, it is of the moment and your two presences meet in that moment. No words are needed. The bond you have forged together over the years is sustained and perpetuated.

Sitting now in the sunlight with the bright music all around us I have an out-of-body experience.

In a waking dream I am suspended somehow above the scene. I see the full dimensions of this small square room. The rectangular bed with Mam wrapped in it and my own figure poised and thoughtful on its edge. There is great energy filling the space around us. Its gold and silver shimmer is suffused with the pure rays of the morning sun.

Above and around me the benevolent ghosts of my aunts and uncles, all in their prime, float silently, witnesses to the nourishing below. I know all of them like yesterday; Roseleen, Betty, Pauline and Maureen, Tim, Frank, and John. And slightly further away a dim shadow of Mam's mam, Elizabeth, ascends. The scene turns sepia, and the pattern of the old wallpaper appears delicately again on the walls. The silver radio is replaced with a much bigger, older set. I am not sitting there any more. Mam is replaced by her mother, similarly wrapped, and all her children stand or sit around her bedside. And sitting there, holding her mother's hand, is a beautiful young woman with dark curled hair – my mother.

My emotion on seeing her so colours the room and the red bow in my mother's hair is the first thing to blush. I know the scene from the telling, though I am sure this vision is my own composition. It is the passing of my granny from consumption. I understand it clearly, though not in any worldly sense. It is a message for me, to me. An echo that reverberates through the past to this present moment. It is a message about the history of my family, the history of this house in Fairview and above all the history contained in these rooms. I see and understand this immediately and clearly because I am of this history, I am the caretaker of this house, a caretaker of our family's history.

Once again, I am sitting in the sunlight on the edge of Mam's bed, feeling now that I am sitting on the edge of her world too. The moment has passed but the message remains. I feel very emotional again and strengthened and comforted beyond any words.

Mam is looking intently at me again. I wonder has she too witnessed the scene just passed. Our eyes meet and I feel inside me the vast sadness I have for Mam return suddenly and with great force. I move quickly from the room to shield her from it, and walk, shaking, to my own, to compose myself and take a few deep breaths. Amidst the few small tears that are forced from me I wonder deeply what this life is all about. Why the past has such a strong emotive effect on me. I have no direct answer, for now.

Deep inside me, though, by way of the pool, I know all the answers wait for me as colours. Words would only make more words. I silently nod my head and my composure returns after a few minutes. I again feel strengthened by the vision. I know I am on the right path doing the right things.

I go back to Mam's room to collect the breakfast things, and see Mam, resting in bed, reading Tony's book again. I look once more around the room and remember a memory of my own. One of my first, from my own earliest personal history, and it too is contained in this room.

4.

Fairview

Our house, an end-of-terrace three-up two-down, has been the family home since it was built in 1927. It was one of over thirteen hundred houses built in the Fairview–Marino area, as part of our fledgling state's first affordable housing scheme. At the time the government allocated the princely sum of one million pounds for the project.

The inspiration for the overall concept of the scheme came from the garden city movement, popular in the early twentieth century. The central idea of the movement was to combine the best parts of city living – schools, shops and other amenities – with the best of country living – green open spaces with plenty of trees, fresh air, and a garden for each house to grow fruit and vegetables in. The plan of the scheme imitated an old design for a formal planned garden for Marino House, which was never initiated. When the work began, all the roadways for the area were laid out following the pathways drawn in the original garden plan.

Keeping true to the spirit of the project, an abundance of green spaces was created among the emerging roads, greens, avenues and terraces. The largest of the spaces, known locally as 'the two circles', are Marino Park and Croydon Park. They sit in the centre of the scheme, anchoring the complex pattern of streets that surround them. There are also triangles, wedges, squares and hexagons of raised green areas, each surrounded by a poured concrete frame. Each green had a stand or two of trees and an access ramp for Dublin Corporation's lawn-mowers. Every house got their gardens too, front and back, of varying dimensions. Each house also had an indoor toilet and running water, both considered a luxury at the time.

Our 'garden city' is framed on all sides by busy thorough-fares. Griffith Avenue and the Malahide Road are to the north and east, with Philipsburgh Avenue and Fairview Strand to the west and south. Fairview church and St Mary's primary school anchor the south-west corner. Old black and white photos of Fairview Strand in the twenties show a long busy row of shops and stores, running from Edges' corner to O'Leary's corner at the far end. Open canvas awnings cover the fronts and shadow the pavement below. Tramlines pass through Fairview coming from the Annesley Bridge Road and carry on out the coast towards Clontarf and Sutton.

On the other side of the tramlines is Fairview Park. Orig-inally a tidal mud flat, the area was used for landfill in the 1900s and rubble from the buildings destroyed during the 1916 Rising was used as part of the fill. In the late twenties playing fields and tree-lined walks were developed and a proper children's playground was built. The park is bound by the Tolka River, which flows into Dublin Bay, on one side and the railway tracks running into Amien Street Station from the north on another.

The legend surrounding our house in Fairview and how it came into our possession involves my grandmother, Elizabeth, called Lizzie. Granny was regarded by all the family as a saint, the first in our family until many years later another came along.

Granny married my grandfather, Francis Rigney, on 21 October 1920 in St Paul's church on Arran Quay. Francis, born in 1881, was eighteen years older than Elizabeth – not an unusual age difference at that time. They had both been born and raised in Dublin; Elizabeth in Chapelizod and Stoney Batter and Francis in the North Strand area. After marrying they lived in Summerhill and East Wall before finally moving to Fairview Green in 1927.

They had nine children between 1921 and 1939, five girls and four boys. Rosanna, known as Roseleen, was the eldest, then came Tim, Frank, Patrick, John, Maureen, Elizabeth, Pauline, and finally Patricia, my mother, the youngest. Patrick died from pneumonia as an infant in 1926.

Francis Rigney worked for the Great Northern Railways (GNR) all his life. Before her marriage Elizabeth worked for the Mercantile Marine Company and had travelled to Liverpool for the firm many times during the First World War.

The family legend goes that when the Fairview–Marino housing scheme was coming together, word got out that eligible residents who lived in the surrounding area would be allocated one of the houses. At the time you needed to have at least three children to be considered eligible for a house. The family were living locally and had the required three children – Rosanna, Tim and Frank. So Granny Lizzie, like a lot of other local ladies, went each day to the on-site office of the foreman to apply 'gentle pressure' on him to allocate her family a house. Eventually the poor man cracked from this pressure, and he rewarded Granny for her perseverance by offering her the pick of the houses just completed. She chose No. 16 and as a result her path to family beatification was guaranteed.

The family moved into Fairview Green in 1927 and the next five children were born during the thirties. Mam was the last, the baby, born on 10 March 1939. It should have been a wonderful time for the family, a brand-new modern home in a well-planned and serviced area, but that was not to be. Francis had a particularly good, well-paid job for the time, but he was a hard-drinking man and a tyrant to the family. Many a night he'd come home late with his cronies to drink in the back room. Aunty Roseleen said it was her job, as the eldest, to watch for him from the upstairs bedroom window each night, in case in his drunkenness he knocked into the wrong house and woke the neighbours. Over the years his children became very adept at leaving the house through the back door as he came in through the front.

Granny was unwell a lot of the time too. She suffered from TB among other things. She often had to 'take to the bed', as they said in those days, and was frequently in and out of hospital. Having nine children in eighteen years did not help her either.

In February 1945 Francis died of a heart attack. His death notice in the *Irish Independent* read, 'Francis, dearly beloved husband of Elizabeth, deeply regretted by his sorrowing wife, sons and daughters.' As nice a line of fiction as you could put together! From that time on, the gloom and fear around the house and family lifted.

The family photos started soon after that time, lovely old black-and-whites. The boys, all tall, handsome and smiling, with Crombies and quiffs, and the girls elegant and gorgeous with beautiful long curly hair and happy faces. Granny is there too among her children looking frail but content and cared for.

Mam, like all her sisters, was sent to Stanhope Street primary school in Stoneybatter for her early education. Granny, who had been brought up in Stoneybatter, had attended there herself. The boys were sent to St Paul's, 'The Brunner', on North Brunswick Street in the same area.

Mam always resented being sent to Stanhope Street, while all her pals just walked around the corner to the local school, St Mary's. It was a long journey each day, she told me many times. Sometimes on the way home Mam would spend her bus fare and buy herself a doughnut. When her doughnut was eaten it was indeed a long walk home.

The discipline in the school was brutal at times. Being slapped hard across the face by a full-grown woman was part of the treatment she and the other girls regularly received. Being publicly humiliated in front of your classmates was another method employed by the 'teachers'.

Even now, writing about that casual violence years later, I feel an anger rising inside me. An anger directed towards these bullies and brutes that had treated Mam so badly. Unfortunately, the treatment was probably on a par with what most kids in Irish schools had to put up with during those times. They were hard years, the forties, for working-class people in Dublin. Dublin 'in the rare oul times' indeed!

Mam survived the school experience and went on to secretarial school to study shorthand and other secretarial skills. When she was fourteen, she was offered her first job. During a class one day a request came in from a solicitor's office on Ormond Quay, looking for a girl to fill a vacancy as an apprentice secretary. Years later, Mam told me, quite proudly, that her teacher had forwarded her name because she was the best in the class. Mam was hired by Frank Tully, who was to be a benevolent employer and much liked by Mam during her time there. As part of her duties, she attended sittings in the Four Courts and took shorthand notes of the proceedings. Mam worked for Mr Tully for ten years, giving up her job to get married, which was the practice at the time. 'They were the happiest days of my life,' she often said.

In 1958 my Mam, aged nineteen, met my father at a dance in the Metropole Ballroom on O'Connell Street. He was a physical training instructor in the army at the time and a couple of years older than Mam. I have a full-length black and white photo, taken shortly after they met, of the two of them walking arm in arm down O'Connell Street. Mam is wearing a dark pencil skirt and fitted jacket and my father is wearing a single-breasted suit with a tie and a knitted cardigan. Both have a Pioneer pin proudly displayed on their left lapels. They look so in step with each other and so happy. I find it a difficult photo to absorb, knowing how things were to unfold in the coming years. But in that moment, they look amazing together, their happiness and potential held for ever inside that little picture frame.

They were married in Fairview church on 17 September 1963. Mam's family were against the marriage and had asked her not to go through with it. 'He'll only be thinking about himself, he'll always be first,' they warned her. She went ahead anyway, as people do when they think they are in love. Mam had already had three or four offers of marriage and had declined them all. She accepted my father's proposal and one of her main reasons for doing so was that he was a Pioneer and did not drink any alcohol. After the family's bad experiences with their own alcoholic father most of them never took a drink in their lives and were not very tolerant of people who did.

The newlyweds moved into Fairview Green to live soon after the wedding. Mam's sister Pauline, who was unmarried, was the only family member still living there at the time. My father had been discharged from the army at this stage and had started working in a school as a physical education teacher. Over the next nine years, from 1964 to 1973, myself and my brothers were born. Tragically, my younger brother Alan was born with leukaemia and died a few weeks after his birth in 1972.

I have no recollection of Alan's passing or the effect it had on my parents' relationship. It did create a rift between them, though, one that would grow over time into a complete fracture. My father had started drinking and had become involved in after-school socialising with the other teachers. He was also starting to resent our close proximity to Mam's family and their influence on her and us.

As a child I was blissfully unaware of all this. Early days in Fairview were happy days. We had lots of good friends and the greens and lanes to play in. There were great neighbours all around us.

All my early memories, the black and white ones, are of the house and its surrounds, with its various rooms and garden providing many a backdrop. My earliest is linked to the room Mam now sleeps in. At the time it was the room we three boys shared.

I was four, and it was the morning of my first day of school. I remember Mam waking me up, something that had never happened in my young life before. Before that morning, I only remember being told to go back to bed, usually because it was too early in the morning or too late at night. Now, here was Mam, my singing angel up to now, pulling back the warm covers and saying things about being late for school and meeting all your new friends and frightening things like that. I resisted getting out of bed until Mam's patience wore out; and then I was hauled up, face washed, packed into my new uniform, and sitting at the breakfast table contemplating my slice of bread and jam, in what felt like one busy minute. I had barely enough time to look into my new school bag, with my books and copies covered in thick wallpaper sitting snugly inside, before my neighbour Kay was at the door to whisk me away. I do remember noticing it was the same wallpaper as on the walls of our sitting room, though!

I bawled when Kay deposited me at my desk in my first high babies' class in St Marys NS. There were other kids bawling and screaming and clinging on to their parents' legs, so I never felt too bad about it. What escaped me, though, was why I was crying at all.

I think now that it is the beginning of the wrench that all young children feel, when the dream world of make believe in which they have very happily existed until now, crashes into the harsher realities of time-keeping, doing what you're told, homework and the subtle dread of having to do it all again tomorrow. Something becomes lost in the collision. Innocence, maybe, the final link to the bliss of the womb. Maybe there's an answer here as to why we spend so much of our later life looking for something or someone to make us feel complete again.

When Kay brought me home after that first trying day, I hid under the dining table and would not come out for ages. I can still see my Mam's legs, skirt below the knee, walking around in her house shoes and hear her encouraging me to come out. I would not, so she eventually left me to it.

I understand now, as a parent myself, why she did so. No matter how bad a job you do parenting your children, they are not going to pack their bags, move out and look for more accommodating parents. Unfortunately, or fortunately, that's not an option open for them.

I eventually crawled out, conceding defeat, and was given a pat on the head by Mam and a piece of raw turnip to chew on, which was, believe it or not, considered a bit of a treat at the time.

Sometime in early 1976 our idyllic childhood in Fairview ended. Things between my father and Mam's family had come to a head and he decided to relocate us and, in the process, attempt to dis-locate us from them. He had rented a big house in Santry for the purpose. Santry at the time was many miles away from Fairview, and on the edge of civilisation as far as we were concerned.

One day we were all packed into our red Renault 16, and we said goodbye to Fairview. It would be 25 years before this hiatus was to end and we would once more move back to live, very happily, in No. 16 again.

5.

AFTER NOON

On a journey home from Wicklow one late autumn evening in 2018, I heard, for the first time, the second movement of Beethoven's fifth piano concerto on the radio. I was so moved I pulled the car over and waited until the very last note had ended. Enveloped by the sound, I was transported away to a deeper place, where I was alone and held within its exquisite melody. I had no desire to breathe and break the spell or to move and lose a single note.

It seemed the music was composed for me, for this moment and how I was feeling. It answered, as a balance, the pain I was suffering from. It was as immense, complex and as personal. I had not realised how unbalanced I was, how far down the pain had gone. That realisation was the light the music had filled me with. The shadows around my confidence in the future were only that, shadows; transparent fears of a small boy holding his mother in his arms.

Sitting at the roadside in the darkened car, I watched the rain slant crossways through the headlights and felt, for the first time, a settling for what had and what would come to pass. It was not over, but for now a measure of my equilibrium was righted. Somehow this genius music transcended my sense and senses, reached in and illuminated a part of me, isolated and foetal in my gloom.

I play it often, summoning its light, to soothe my jangled nerves and to ease the ache and strain I feel in my body. I wonder did the maestro compose it as a response to some personal turmoil or to his own need for some healing light. This human condition is indeed ageless. I like to imagine he and I have something in common; the music at least says as much.

It is now after noon and the second part of my day is upon me. The morning, with its fixing and nourishing, has passed. In the time between the two there are chores to do.

The laundry is a constant. With two, sometimes three or four, young ladies in the house, our washing machine is always on the go. Mam's clothes, her bed linen and the pile of necessary towels queue patiently with the rest. My own meagre wardrobe gets shunted repeatedly by the more important gym gear, tonight's outfit or the unreasonable amount of pyjamas and nightwear.

The current bout of fine weather is a godsend and in the recent days our back garden has resembled a county fair. We have the full clothesline, colourfully dancing in the breeze, and the more mobile clothes horses, limbs open wide, festooned with all sorts of tops, bottoms, odds and ends, placed and moved around the garden depending on the angle of the sun.

There is usually a daughter or two sunning themselves among it all. Their music, always playing close to the ground, adds atmosphere to the fair. I admire their perseverance baking away there in the sun. I never had the patience for it.

The house also needs to be kept in shape and we all carry out the various household tasks with varying levels of enthusiasm. The situation with Mam and our necessary daily routine is a presence and adds into this; sparks can occasionally fly over trivia. We manage collectively to wipe this slate clean each morning and do not allow these moments to fester. We know and love each other too well for it to be otherwise.

A large amount of good humour is also required and thankfully we all naturally possess a good measure of it. Attempting to clamber onto one's high horse around here would bring a heap of ridicule down on top of you. In this emotional atmosphere, humour is the best emotion of all.

Chores done, I find myself sitting in front of the TV mindlessly flicking through the channels. It is time to begin the next part of the day, but my body will not move from the chair. My mind is willing and is ready to go but can do nothing without the co-operation of the mass. I understand this phenomenon very well. In the bar trade we call it the 'the two hard yards moment'.

In most bars or public houses, the front door is usually located within a couple of yards of the bar counter. If you have been supping for a while, enjoying the company and the craic, there comes that time when you have to leave.

When it comes, for some people the body is willing, but their mind knows that what waits for them outside the door is rarely as pleasant as sitting here with a pint at their elbow. For some, the mind is willing, but the body is not capable of responding. I have watched many people struggle to get across the 'two hard yards' from their stool at the counter and on out the front door into the night. If they can make it across and out, they are not worried about walking any distance after that to get home. Some people will lurch and nearly throw themselves out through the door. Others lose the battle momentarily and turn in their stool for one last round.

I am at my two hard yards moment and manage, figuratively, to throw myself through the door and begin the climb to the central part of my day. Once I have made the decision, all my focus is now on the task ahead. The mind settles into the rhythm, and I prepare to begin the routine as if it were for the first time.

Upstairs I check Mam to see where she is at. This morning she is focusing on the subtitles to one of her movies. I enter the bedroom and she fixes me with her gaze. I have her attention.

'Well, Mam, will we get up and go downstairs for something to eat?' I ask in a cheerful tone from the foot of her bed. No response. I am watching her expression and wait for a gleam or a little nod of her head.

I hear an echo from my friend Des, 'You cannot do this from the outside; you must go into her world, see things as she does.' I try again, speaking slowly, clearly and a little louder, trying to bring her closer to the surface of her understanding.

'Would you like to come down and have something to eat, Mam?' No response, but Mam is still watching me. She knows the words and my tone, it's slowly sinking in.

'Will we get up, go downstairs, and have something to eat, would that be okay?' She is here. I can see it in her eyes, a moment's focus. She nods her head slightly once and then again. We are in this moment together.

'Right so,' I carry on, partially closing the curtains for privacy, before turning down the duvet to below her feet. Our dog

Scamp (his name and his nature), now buried there beneath its folds, pokes out his head. If he could wear a watch, I'm sure at this moment he would be checking the time. Little rascal!

'Do you want to swing your legs out of bed there?' I ask a couple of times,

'Swing your legs out there, swing your legs out there,' Mam says slowly, quietly.

She starts to move, and I help by gently lifting and turning her legs, then clasping her hands and gently pulling until she is sitting on the edge of the bed.

I give her a moment to gather herself and go to the bathroom to put a shape on it. I have showered Mam a thousand times and begin to put the right things in the right place and in the right way. Door to walk-in shower opened back, shower seat and handles down, face cloth hanging over handrail, two floor towels in place, shampoo and body wash perched on the sink, toilet seat up, wipes in place, light and extractor fan on, window closed, a quick double check and I am back with Mam in a couple of minutes. *Look at your watch now, Scamp,* I say to myself.

Back in the room Mam waits patiently. I remind myself again that it is Mam I am dealing with, and this thought allows me to stay centred and in the moment with her. If you are not being present, frustration and impatience can seep into the task.

'It's not her fault, she's trying her best,' I constantly remind myself.

From the radio the first notes of the adagio from Joaquín Rodrigo's seminal 'Concierto de Aranjuez' glide into the room. I turn up the volume a little on the little silver herald by the bed.

'Now, Mam, put your left hand here and your right hand here.' I place Mam's hand crossways on to the bottom edge of her pyjama top, and she grips the ends. I reach around behind her and with both hands begin to lift her pyjamas and vest together in a much-practised movement.

'Now, Mam, one, two, three, let's lift together.' We do and in one swift movement the top is off.

'We're going to stand up now, Mam.' I take her outstretched hands, gripping hand and wrist together.

'Okay, one, two, three, lift.' I lean back and pull gently. Mam's up on steady legs, stronger than this morning, I note.

I give her a moment to check her balance.

'Right now, let's take a small step.' She does.

'That's it, one step at a time.' After the first hesitant step she is surer and takes another.

We carry on with our twenty steps to the bathroom accompanied by Rodrigo and his guitar. The concierto reminds me of some of the westerns we have watched together over the years. *The Searchers*, *Rio Bravo*, *True Grit*; John Wayne was always her favourite.

We make it to the bathroom, and I lower Mam's clothes and slowly turn her to sit on the loo. She creaks and bends again and settles. I remove her things.

Again, it is Mam I am dealing with; there are two of us in this situation. I try to remain in the moment and breath very easy now. I know the task, each step, and its purpose. There is no need for hurry or impatience. I know that my energy, positive or negative, can transfer to Mam and if I can control it, it will be a better, calmer experience for both of us.

'That was handy enough,' I say, looking into her eyes. She nods slowly, wondering what I mean.

I give her a couple of minutes to herself.

Back in her room I quickly remake her bed and drape a big towel neatly down its side. I take talcum powder, moisturiser, deodorant, and the multi-purpose Silcock's base from the drawer of her dresser and line them up on top of it. I bring another big towel to the landing for drying afterwards.

I pop my head around the bathroom door again. 'Are you happy enough now, Mam?' I ask two, three times, waiting for her response.

'I'm happy enough,' she nods eventually.

I walk in, closing the door behind me, turn on the shower and prepare some loo roll for Mam.

'Now, when you're ready,' I take Mam's offered hands. 'One, two, three, and stand up.' She does, uses the roll, and we take a couple of small steps towards the running shower with its steam rising.

I guide her hands onto the supports and take the shower head down and spray the seat and back rest to heat them up a little.

'Now, Mam, hold on to that side rail, that's it, take a few steps in, I'll just heat up the seat for you.'

Mam ducks under the outstretched shower hose, brushes the excess water off the seat and very carefully steps in, turns herself around and sits down with a little splash!

I breathe easier and let the warm jet of water over her body for a minute to get some of its heat into her.

'Is that water alright? It's not too hot for you, Mam?' I ask a few times, moving the jet all over.

'The water's alright, the water's alright,' she finally answers, head bowed.

I proceed with well-practised movements, soaping and rinsing, chatting with Mam all the time. Sometimes I will sing a few words from one of her old favourites or whistle a familiar melody, attempting to bring some normality and everydayness into an experience that neither of us ever thought likely.

The smooth crooning voice of the gentle Nat King Cole fills my head with the words to 'Straighten Up and Fly Right'. He was a firm favourite of Mam's and the lyrics splash and jive with the hot water and steam.

Back, front, legs, rinse her hair, she washes her face, she stands, I rinse her down and we are done. It might have taken all of ten minutes. I don't hurry. I believe the warm water is beneficial to Mam. Its touch invigorates all her cells and washes away yesterday. I spend a good minute letting the jets through her hair, massaging her scalp. I imagine it stimulates and awakens what lies beneath.

'Now, that's it, Mam,' I say, turning off the shower. 'I'll just get you a nice towel.' I step from the warm steam on to the landing, half showered myself by the spray.

Back with the large dry towel, I offer one end to Mam. 'Now grab the end of that towel, Mam, and give your face a dry. Both hands.' She does and buries her face in the towel.

I dry her legs and her forearms and put the towel over her head to dry her back and then finally her hair and behind her ears. Again, it is a well-rehearsed series of moves and takes a couple of minutes. Mam sits up now and I brush the hair from her face back behind her ears. Her eyes are a little red from the water, but she looks and sounds more present and refreshed.

'Now dry your arms and under your arms. Yes, that's it,' I add encouragingly.

'Under your arms, under your arms,' she echoes. 'It's very important, it's very important,' she adds in a nice little ad lib. She is here alright, trying to make the best out of it as she has always done. It brings my heart into my mouth, these little glimpses of her old self. They can humble me and encourage me too.

She finishes drying her upper body and I ask her to sit forward while I place the towel over her shoulders. She clasps the two sides together around her and with her right hand holds the handrail in preparation for standing up.

'Right so, are you ready to get out of here and get dressed?' She nods a couple of times. I move beside her and give her a steadying lift as she carefully stands up. I take her hands in mine, and we retrace our twenty steps again, leaving the bathroom and its warm watery mess for later.

In the bedroom we slow pirouette and I land Mam squarely in the middle of the draped towel placed across her bed. I quickly wrap her legs in its dryness and give her a moment to gather herself.

'That went well love, didn't it?' I ask, then, 'We'll have you dressed in a flash. You can't go walking around in your birthday suit now, can you?'

'In your birthday suit, in your birthday suit,' she chimes back, and we both smile at each other. Yes, she is there alright. Such a salve for the spirit is this unlooked-for and unexpected smile. Another reward for my presence and the decision I made a long time ago.

I unwrap her legs and with a third, smaller towel thoroughly dry them and her feet. I talc her feet for extra dryness and moisturise her legs, arms and upper body. Mam is great during all this, sitting calmly and responding positively to all my requests and directions. I think sometimes she is a little bemused by it all.

'I'm just going to put some cream on your back, Mam, and then we're nearly done.' She nods as I walk around the bed and sit down behind her.

'Going to put some cream on your back, going to put some cream on your back,' follows me.

The Silcock's base is extremely useful and effective. There have been many skin issues over the last couple of years and Silcock's has had all the answers. I spread it on liberally.

With that stage completed I spray a little deodorant and place all my four assistants back into their little drawer.

'Right so, that's all finished, let's get some clothes on you now.'

Mam is sitting watching me closely from the edge of the bed, with half-dry hair and skin gleaming from the creams. For the hundredth time I wonder what she is thinking. I brush back the hair from forehead and eyes and ask her if she is all right.

She nods and looking closely into the dark pupil of her eye, I notice a very tiny, perfect, reflection of myself captive there. It is difficult to express the impression this has on me. I falter momentarily. Who am I? What gives me the right to be doing this? What is Mam thinking? What is the point of all this caring?

I breathe deeply, once, twice and regain control of myself; this is not the time for these questions or for finding any answers to them. They can surface at any time, swirling around inside my head like flapping crows around a bell tower, uninvited, spreading discord through my ordered mind.

It passes in a heartbeat, exhaled. It is like another test of my resolve and purpose. I pass for now and realise I'm still kneeling before my mother looking into her eyes. She looks back with her familiar patience. Somehow, I feel reassured. I am doing the right thing. Keep going, stay in the moment; stay with Mam in this moment. I stand, breathe easier and carry on.

'Now, let's get these pants on you. That's it, right foot first, then the next one.' Mam helps, lifts her feet in turn and I bring her safety pants up to her knees.

'Now we'll stand up, Mam. Right hand here, I'll hold your left and one, two, three, stand.' She does, with her right hand on the dresser, and turns slightly as I put her left hand there too. I pull up the safeties and sit her down again.

I take a clean vest from her tall dresser, pop it over her head, she puts her arms through, and I twist and straighten it. I select a shirt from her clothes rail and help her on with it. I button the sleeves and the top three buttons and ask Mam to fasten the rest.

While she is doing that, I quickly go back into the bathroom and leave it like I found it thirty minutes ago. It takes a minute or two and I return to Mam's room.

Mam is studying Tony's memorial card that we keep on her bedside locker. She is reading the small print beneath the full-length picture of him, smiling on his visit to the Convento di Assisi in Umbria, Italy, many years ago.

I am aboard a fast train with only one stop. I'm not in a mad hurry to disembark. I'm like everyone else: I only know this life, but I see no meaning in this life ending in a grave. When the train stops, I will step onto the platform with hope and no fear.

I busy myself in the room, giving her the moment, until she replaces the card. She sits quietly and no hint of what she is feeling or thinking escapes her. It is a measure of how far this illness has taken her, enveloped her, swallowed her. It is beyond disturbing and opens again the vast ache that becomes a part of you when you are living with a loved one and this illness.

Action again is the temporary tonic and I pull back from this abyss to the moment, to the now. I select her light green trousers and again we left foot, right foot, stand, twist, tuck in and sit again.

'We're nearly there, Mam,' I say, putting on her socks and then her shoes.

I fasten on Mam's necklace and then her watch. The battery stopped in it many months ago. It is symbolic of where we are at. We are on our own time now and Mam doesn't read it any more, but she still likes to wear it.

I pull back the curtains again and open the window wide. The room fills with light and the sounds of the world outside. I take another minute to put the room back in order.

'Would you eat a small bowl of porridge, Mam?' I ask a couple of times as I move around the room.

'I would eat a small bowl of porridge,' she replies. 'Only a small bowl,' she adds from under her eyebrows – she has not forgotten everything!

At the top of the stairs, folded neatly, is the chair for the stairlift. It was installed three years ago at the same time we had the bathroom converted. Mam refused to use it until about four months ago. It showed something of her character and independence that she insisted on walking up and down the stairs unassisted, despite its presence. I never objected and going up and down three or four times a day was good exercise for her. I would walk behind her or in front of her, depending on which way she was going. It only takes a moment to have a fall and I was always very watchful.

Then one day her legs were shaking too much as she was coming down and she sat down on the stairs and would not move. It took an age to help her down that day. It was another sad indicator of her decline. Since then, the chair has become her chariot. It has taken quite a while for her to relax when she is on it. Each time seems to her like her first and, like all the other little things, I use the same words and tone each time she uses it.

I turn it on and fold down the seat and arms and return to Mam's room to fetch her.

'Now, Mam, will we go down and have something to eat?' I ask, taking her hands. I lean back and pull gently and slowly she stands rights herself and takes a small step. On the landing she holds the top of the stairs and I edge her onto the seat.

'Hoosh yourself back a bit, that's it, I'll just put on this seat belt. Now, the chair will turn and then it will go down, okay?'

Mam nods. I push the control, the chair beeps, whirrs and turns before descending. Mam grabs the staircase rail and goes hand over hand all the way down to the hall. I follow her down.

'Hang on there a sec, Mam,' I say, stepping past her.

I go into the front room and plug in the hairdryer. Usually, one of the girls is around to do Mam's hair but for today I am her stylist, God help her!

I unbuckle her, take her hands and we walk into the salon, really the front room, and Mam swivels and eases down onto the black leather office chair. As I blow-dry her hair, she is very relaxed. It is such a familiar, comforting thing for her. For most of her recent years Mam had her hair done each Saturday morning. I know myself how relaxing it can be getting your hair cut. You are where you are meant to be, you've nothing else to do or to be doing and someone is taking care of you. I can see all this on Mam's face as she sits peacefully with her eyes closed.

Job done, I check my work. Satisfied, I hand her a comb for her to finish the styling.

I go into the back room and make sure her chair and table are ready for her 'lunch'. I switch on the cable box and the TV. Then I go to the kitchen and fill a small pot with a cup of water and add to it a handful plus a touch more of organic porridge oats. I put it on the gas on a low heat and go back for Mam.

She looks good, with her hair in shape, and with our practised one, two, three get her up off the chair, slow step into the back room and drop her down easy to the next chair. It is a nice big comfortable armchair with a retractable footrest. A cushion behind her back keeps her up straight for her porridge.

The porridge is bubbling nicely, taking only a minute to dissolve in the warm water. I pour it into a bowl, add a drop of cooling milk and a teaspoon of brown sugar. It needs the sugar! I bring a chair into the room and sit on Mam's right side, stirring the porridge to blend it all and to take some of the heat out of it.

The health and nutritional benefits of oatmeal are well documented. The fact that many tons of it is consumed each day in our hospitals and nursing homes is testament to that fact. It contains lots of protein, antioxidants and soluble fibres, which are great for the tummy. It also leaves you feeling warm and full, which also helps.

I spread a napkin under her chin and offer her a small spoonful as a temperature check.

'That's not too hot for you, love, is it?' She shakes her head a little and returns her gaze to the telly. *Escape to the Country* is on, a family favourite. *Escape from the country*, I'm thinking, as I slowly feed Mam warm spoonfuls of nourishment. Mam swallows it down, enjoying it. Another familiar experience for her while she sits in her own home on her own chair. In a few moments the porridge is gone and with a large mouthful of water to wash it down my task is complete. 'That'll keep her going for a while', I say to myself, wiping her mouth, and I take everything back to the kitchen.

On the TV the middle-aged couple are looking at a small mansion in the English Cotswolds. He likes it, but his opinion doesn't matter if his wife doesn't. She doesn't. They move on to the mystery house, and I move too to the back garden for some healing sunlight with Beethoven's Fifth whispering in my ear.

6.

Hiatus

Our family moved to Santry Close in 1976. I was seven years old and unaware of the reasons for the move. As a child I didn't see too far in front of me and never thought to look over my shoulder. What I did see was that we were now living in a much bigger house and that I had a bedroom of my own for the first time.

The Close was surrounded by farmland. Over the low back wall, at the end of our long, wide garden, fields of corn stretched in all directions. Over the years these fields were to be a wonderful playground and hideaway for myself and my brothers. After the harvest, the farmer would bale the straw and we would build elaborate forts with the bales, hurling the stumps of corn and muck, like grenades, at each other. Santry woods, across the Swords road, were wild and unkempt at the time and we had many adventures there too. We had some lovely neighbours on both sides of us and in the houses around. We had friends to make and play with too.

It was quite different from the Fairview we had grown up in; it was also a long way from there. It was not easy for Mam to get around or to stay in contact with her family. Most families at the time had only one car, if that, and the men were the ones driving them. I can remember us having to walk everywhere; to the local shops beside the original Swiss Cottage, or to Whitehall church, which, on my short legs, seemed many miles away.

Mam was not happy. The isolation and dislocation from her roots and family was a terrible experience for her. Relations between her and our father worsened. My first indication that something was amiss was when I returned from a summer stint in the Gaeltacht in Falcarragh, County Donegal in 1979. I'd spent four weeks there learning how to smoke cigarettes, dance to 'The Walls of Limerick' and hold hands with my very first girlfriend. Back in the house in Santry I noticed that the television was missing. As I looked more closely I saw that other items of furniture were also missing.

A couple of weeks later my father called me into his upstairs bedroom. He was getting dressed, threading his belt into his trousers. It was a strange experience and one usually fraught with an element of danger. He started to explain that things were not going well between himself and Mam and that 'it' was over. He kept dressing as he spoke, casually, as if he was speaking to an acquaintance. He might have been talking about the weather for all I took in. I was waiting for the punchline and a shout or slap. When he finished talking, I said 'Okay' and left the room wondering what that was all about.

A couple of minutes later my friends knocked at the front door and asked if I wanted to go to the pictures with them.

I was halfway through explaining that I had no money to go when my father appeared on the landing and offered me the money to go. Now I was alarmed. That was out of character for him and more disturbing for me than his effort at explaining things earlier.

One morning, a couple of months later, Mam and my brothers and I moved to another house at the end of the street. I can still see myself looking through the net-curtained window of my new upstairs bedroom at my friends calling for me at our old house – the houses were that near to each other.

The new house was a semi, built at the small keyhole end of the road and facing up the Close. It was another three-up, two-down but was fifty years younger than our home in Fairview. It had larger rooms and a set of sliding doors separating the front room from the back room. The kitchen was bigger too, with a table and chairs where we could eat our meals.

In the side garden our new landlord kept his old wooden boat on a trailer. The long back garden with a clothesline and a concrete path down its centre was dug into rows and primed for planting potatoes. It was a great landscape for a young boy with a keen interest in toy soldiers and the imagination to go with it. Over the back wall ran a stream with a narrow pathway all along its length and overshadowed by trees and plants, an even better hideaway and playground where expensive toys were not required.

Our world had been turned upside down and it was to take quite a while before it righted itself into a new and different pattern. Mam was free, though, and her laughter and singing could be heard once more around our new home. Us boys did not make it easy for her, of course! Our auntie Pauline was always calling us brats, and she was right most of the time.

Mam had to work part time now to make ends meet. Predictably, our selfish father did not do much to help. I think his ego took a battering when Mam left him; he made it hard for her and us, and contested everything. We saw him once a week on a Sunday for few hours, and we were always glad when we were returned home.

My memories of our three years in this house are sparse and without colour. I hold them now at arm's length or quickly glance at them, not wanting to see any of the details. They are also quiet memories, silent ones. My experience of these days has deliberately removed the sound from them. Gratefully, now, I close that album and all the moments it contains. I don't live in the past any more – surviving it was enough.

Our seven years in Santry ended on my fourteenth birthday. In October 1982 we moved again, this time to the parish of Iona in Glasnevin. We had the first house on the street with a narrow access lane at one side and the Smurfit printing works looming large over the back wall. We now had the local shop right across the road and the parish church of St Columba only a short walk around the corner.

I remember walking with Mam up the long, tree-lined Hollybank Road, for my first visit to the house. I was miserable, thinking of another set of friends and familiar places I would be leaving behind. In the new house, wandering through the empty rooms together, Mam said that we would be all right, that it would all work out. I wasn't convinced. I had become quite wild over the Santry years, making the most of its open landscape and country playgrounds. Iona was a very settled neighbourhood. There were no more streams and fields where I could escape from the house and my brothers. It seemed hemmed in by comparison, more industrial and built-upon.

Mam was right in the end, though. It was not long before new friends were found and some of them were even girls.

Iona church was to play a large part in Mam's life over the next years. She always had a strong faith and often said that without that faith she would not have found the strength to keep going. One of our neighbours, the formidable Mrs Valentine, who was a music teacher, played the organ and was the lead in the church choir. Once she heard Mam singing in her beautiful, sweet voice it was not long before she had encouraged her to join the choir. Through the choir Mam met and made a lot of new friends. Like most gifts, her singing ability was the key that opened those doors of friendship. Her past and her circumstances were not what she was judged by, and she flourished in the friendly and understanding company.

Her family continued to be a great support too. Auntie Pauline was a frequent visitor. She adopted the role of a second parent and was always hassling us to cut the grass, do our chores and, memorably, to return the empty glass lemonade bottles to the shop to collect the few pence they gave you for doing so. Many a time I would escape over the back wall, into the lane behind, when I heard or saw her coming. It was like a mirroring of what my uncles used to do in Fairview during the forties to escape their father.

Our aunts and uncles were regular visitors. They continued to be a comforting constant in what had become a difficult few years. Uncle Frank was a lovely man, kind and gentle and with a great affection for Mam. I can still recall him in the house putting up the curtains in the back room while he was on his lunch break. Uncle Tim was called in when we were giving more trouble than usual. He was tough and a straight talker. Always, though, his wife, our lovely Auntie Kathleen, was there too, playing the good cop to Tim's bad one. They were a great double act and I always remember Kathleen's gentleness and understanding towards me.

Mam started to travel more, usually with her sisters. Auntie Betty was the great organiser of the trips. The colourful brochures she brought to show Mam were very exotic with their beaches, blue skies, and glimpses of faraway places. We had never travelled abroad as a family and we all took our turn flicking through the pages dreaming of aeroplanes, palm trees and shimmering swimming pools.

Not all their holidays and trips away were to the sunshine, though. Mam and all the aunties were regulars on the pilgrimages, usually organised by the parish church, to Lourdes, Nevers or to Međugorje. There was always a big turnout in the parish for these trips. All the pilgrims would meet outside the church on the morning of departure and pose for a group photo under the colourful banner of the Church of Columba, Iona.

Mam was also working again. After a year or so in Iona, Tony, now aged nineteen, was working in Finglas, at the General Medical Services, which everyone called the GMS. When a vacancy came up there for a new canteen lady Mam's name was mentioned, possibly by our neighbour Helen Valentine, the daughter of Mrs Valentine, possibly by Tony, or maybe both. Mam got the job and worked there for nearly ten years.

Mam's duties, which involved breaks and lunch service, were light enough. Lots of pots of tea were required. And, as everyone knows, Mam loved her tea. Mam was remembered there for her kindness and her great sense of humour. Her pride in the Dublin football team was also on show. After a Dublin victory in Croke Park Mam would head out towards the stadium and return with scarves and flags with which to decorate the canteen on the following Monday morning. It all made for good banter with her country colleagues. When people were feeling low or had a problem Mam was always a kind and wise confidante, speaking from her experience in her non-judgemental way.

Over the next few years our family started to grow up and to break up. The priesthood and emigration, the classic Irish story, were to claim my first two brothers. When I turned seventeen it was my turn to spread my wings and make the move to flatland and my first attempt at independence. I had managed to remain in school to complete my Leaving Cert, and I passed it too, scraping over the brow of acceptable grades, close enough to leave some skin behind me.

My bedsit was halfway down Clonliffe Road with Croke Park Stadium over my back wall. It was hardly the other side of the globe, but it was a start. Mam said, with what I like to remember were tears in her eyes, that I would regret moving out.

I certainly did on my first night there. My friends had helped me carry down my few meagre possessions and then left late in the evening to go home to their nice comfortable houses. As I surveyed my new kingdom from my single bed, I realised I'd no TV, no radio and no kettle. My little fridge was empty, and I didn't have a 50p coin for the electricity meter.

This was the first clear separation between my pathway and Mam's. A rite of passage we all go through in one way or another. As you make that change your own life and pathway come to the fore, necessarily so. Over the next three years I moved back and forth between the house in Iona and Mam, and my own place in the world, in ever-widening circles. I moved to the Greek islands the following summer for a few weeks and stayed five months in the sunshine before returning home. London was next, the following spring; then back to the islands for another five months.

In the summer of 1989, I again moved to London, this time with my partner and another classic Irish scenario. My partner was pregnant, but we were not married, did not have a house of our own and in the Ireland of the time this was still shameful for the family. We told no one and saved up the money to travel to London to stay with my partner's sister.

I can still remember standing in the red phone box on Blackstock Road in Highbury, London, one November evening a few months later, ringing home and Mam answering the phone.

'Hi, Mam, it's Kieran, how are you?'

'Hi, Kieran, I'm fine, I'm just back from Mass. It's late to call, is everything all right?'

'Yeah, yes, everything is okay. I have some news for you though, ehm …' And after taking months to rehearse my lines for this especially important call I blurted out, 'Mandi is pregnant!'

There was silence on the other end of the line, but only for a moment.

'I thought she might be,' she answered, in that all-knowing motherly way. 'When is she due, do you think?' she asked, very calmly and kindly.

'At Christmas time, Mandi reckons, sometime in the middle or near the end of December.'

'A Christmas baby. That'll be nice. Are you okay for everything?'

Such a relief to hear her sweet voice down the line. No accusations, no thought for herself and what people would say. She had had enough of that in her own life. Just kindness and understanding, two of the many pillars that supported who this lady was. I shed some tears when I hung up the phone, mostly of relief, but I was deeply touched by Mam's concern for us, for her looking beyond the words and seeing us for what we were.

Our daughter Jasmyn was born on 21 December in Seven Sisters maternity hospital. It was quite an experience, but my daughter has banned me from relating it here. Mam was one of our first visitors and she stayed for some days to help us settle. Jasmyn was Mam's first grandchild too. I can still see her sitting in our front room beside the Christmas tree, wearing her full-length red dressing gown, rocking Jasmyn to sleep, singing lightly in her lovely voice.

We were back in Dublin in less than two years. London had been a very difficult time for us, and it felt good to be back home again. The next few years were quite turbulent for me and our young family. We moved from house to house each year, with more baggage each time. On 1 June 1993, our second daughter Khloe was born. I delivered Khloe myself in the house we were sharing with my cousin and our friends on St Philomena's Road in Glasnevin. We were remarkably lucky that there were no complications with Khloe's birth. It was an amazing and frightening experience, especially for Mandi. I have often told the story but again have been banned from telling it here.

We moved again, then again, Phibsboro, Drumcondra, and then Drumcondra again. We were never too far from Iona and Mam.

Our final move as a family was to the village of Laragh in County Wicklow. It was to be a fresh start for us, away from the city and its influences. It is a beautiful part of the country with hills and forest walks. There was silence in the evenings and wood smoke in the air. You could watch the rain drift down the valley from Glendalough and stand out in the clouds as it washed across you.

In the end it was too quiet and lonely in the evenings for a city boy. I missed the noise, the activity of the city. There was no sound of trains shunting across the valley or foghorns from the ships in the Dublin Bay. I never realised how comforting the familiar sounds around me were until they were not there anymore. In the end, it was too much for us and for the unsteady platform we had tried to build our family on. Yeats, in words and emotion, encapsulated the turmoil, wrench and pain I felt and felt I had helped to cause.

Turning and turning in the widening gyre
The falcon cannot hear the falconer;
Things fall apart; the centre cannot hold;
Mere anarchy is loosed upon the world,
The blood-dimmed tide is loosed, and everywhere
The ceremony of innocence is drowned;
The best lack all conviction, while the worst
Are full of passionate intensity.

There's a sense of history repeating itself, another family break-up, but this one I am fully aware of; I am in the centre of it. This time I'm the one standing in the empty house wondering where it all went wrong. The feeling was beyond pain. There was a place within myself that I could not escape from. I was on my knees and badly wounded. I needed a refuge to try and recover myself, find myself amongst the pieces scattered on the ground at my feet. I went home again, to my centre, to Iona and Mam.

Today, whenever I get frustrated with my daily routine, or complain to myself about how things have worked out, I remember this period of my life and that the only bright shining light that was there for me at the time was Mam.

She was as disappointed as I was, but she did not reproach me for the mess I had made of things. I moved back into my room, the girls came to stay three days a week and we got on with life. We found a new routine. Our paths were running side by side again and would continue to do so, continually, till the present day.

Mam's older sister Pauline had continued to live in Fairview Green. Born in 1936, she was two and a half years older than Mam. Pauline had always taken great care of Mam. She was strong and independent, had never married and never regretted not doing so. She was a constant in our lives and Mam and her were the best of friends. We often went to Bewley's Café on Westmoreland Street, where Pauline worked, when we were children. We would sit around one of the high tables and Pauline would bring over pots of tea and plates of cream cakes and doughnuts for us to munch on. It was a rare treat to be sitting there with cream on our faces and our legs swinging beneath our chairs. Such a happy memory.

Sometime in late 1998 tragedy was to strike close to home and very close to Mam's heart. One day Mam and Tony called to Pauline's for a late breakfast. Pauline was always very organised and reliable. But that morning she burned the beans and did not realise that she had done so. Mam and Tony were very alarmed – this kind of thing just did not happen at Pauline's! Tragically, this was one of the first symptoms of the onset of dementia. The family were devastated. Pauline, who had been such a rock, was the first member of the family to contract this terrible disease. Unfortunately, she was not to be the last.

Her decline into the illness was rapid and frightening. This was a new person we were dealing with, a strong, fully grown woman in the prime of her physical health. Pauline had never been ill before. Mam was deeply upset, and Tony too – he was always her favourite. Within a year Pauline was safely in High Park nursing home, a place where she had worked as a receptionist for many years up until her illness. She had a lot of great friends working there. It was close to Fairview and easy for the family to visit.

Fairview Green was empty now. Soon after, Mam, my two young daughters and I returned to live there once more. It had taken us twenty-five years but finally our 'hiatus' was over, and we were very happily home once again.

7.

WALKS AND DRIVES

In the weeks leading up to Mam's eightieth birthday, I selected from the family archives eighty random photos of her and put them around the walls of our downstairs rooms and hallway. As Mam's illness has progressed, a sense of her identity slipping away has been growing in my mind. I put the photographs up because I want to remind everyone who calls to the house what Mam's presence has meant to so many different people over the years.

Looking now at the broad arc of her life, constants and patterns emerge from the images. The most poignant is Mam's beautiful smile. In the earliest photo, a head and shoulders black-and-white taken in 1955, when she was sixteen, Mam smiles and her whole face smiles. Her eyes are bright and engaged, her cheeks wide and slightly dimpled, her face uplifted towards the camera. In the most recent photo, taken a week before her eightieth birthday, all these characteristics are still vividly on display.

Another constant is colour. Mam in a full-length blue and white dress with matching broad-brimmed hat at my brother's wedding in Australia. Mam in a dark green high-necked dress posing with Tony in our back garden in Iona, their arms comfortably around each other's waists. Wearing pink with my cousin Frank, Mam's godson and a firm favourite. In a lemon-yellow singlet and matching skirt sitting easy on a wooden boat with the blue Mediterranean Sea shining behind her. And Mam in her much later years in a striped purple and mauve cardigan, microphone in hand, singing at the ladies' club in Fairview. Mam could wear any colour; they all enhanced her warmth, beauty and sense of style.

There are lots of photos of Mam on holidays in various parts of the world. In Canada with her dear friend Pat McCarthy and Pat's daughter Brenda. All wearing see-through raincoats on a boat beneath the Niagara Falls. In Australia, happily feeding a kangaroo in an outdoor centre for indigenous wildlife. Dressed in all white smiling beneath a plinthed statue of Mozart in Vienna. On the steps of the Pantheon in Rome clutching a light cardigan and the thin straps of her handbag. In the bright sunshine of Spain laughing with her sister Betty. In all the photos Mam's smile is present and her style and sense of colour on display.

And our family, of course, the most important and constant of all the elements in Mam's life. There is a group shot of Mam and her sisters, taken in the early nineties, on the steps of Buswells hotel in Dublin, with her American cousins and their children. And another with all her brothers and sisters, years later, with nieces and nephews in the gaps between and sitting at their feet. With Roseleen and Pauline in Iona, Mam's hand resting lightly on her eldest sister's shoulder, a touching gesture that is repeated in other photos. Laughing with Pauline, her closest and dearest sister, with whom Mam had hoped to grow old together in their later years. With Tony, in his mid-twenties, smiling together in the back garden and another later one, sitting on Tony's lap at a party laughing aloud together, each so much a part of the other.

My mind swirls as I take them all in, and again that sadness for the way things are wells inside and echoes across my brimming pool. In reflection, all these things are ending or have ended. Many of the family and friends in the photos have passed and gone. Mam will not be travelling carefree in this world any more, and now I am dressing her, and in my emotional state all the real colour has been washed out of my world.

As a counterbalance and a single silver bell chiming in my gloom, Mam's beautiful smile remains. It seems to come from somewhere deep inside her, making her whole face light up and the mask of her illness momentarily disappear. It gives me a glimmer of hope that we will always be together in this world or in the worlds beyond.

'Will we go for a spin?' Mam says from her comfortable armchair, breaking my heavy reverie. Our eyes meet and we smile together.

'We will,' I answer. 'Where would you like to go?'

'Will we go out the coast?' She smiles.

'We will,' I smile back. 'Just give me a minute to get organised.'

It has been our afternoon routine for these many months, something we both enjoy and an opportunity to get out of the house and its certain atmosphere for a while. It's movement too, for both of us, physical and stimulating, a good contrast to the endless wondering and hoping that can become too much on this metaphysical journey we are sharing together.

I load Mam's folding wheelchair into the back of the car, leaving the doors open to allow some of the day's heat to escape from inside. Add cushions and blankets in case of a strong coastal breeze and step back inside to retrieve Mam.

She is still sitting, still watching the telly, the thought of a drive forgotten.

'Will we go for a spin, Mam?' I ask as a gentle reminder. 'We'll go out the coast?'

'That'd be nice,' she finally answers, dragging her attention from the images on the screen.

'Do you need to go to the loo?' Parenting the parent again.

If Mam needs to, we will go through the routine of the chairlift and bathroom as before and proceed from there. Here is where patience and understanding really come into play. Patience because it is important that Mam is comfortable and fresh sitting in the car for the next couple of hours, and it is worth taking the time to make sure. Understanding because it is not about me and how I view time. We are on Mam's time, and remembering that allows me to stay calm and in the moment with her.

We are good to go today.

I stand in front of Mam, brace my legs, and offer her both my hands.

'Now give me your hands, dear, and we'll stand up.' Mam does so.

'Okay, one, two, three, lift.' I lean back and Mam, with a little effort and creaking knees, slowly stands.

'Okay, that went well, now take a minute to find your feet.' When she's taken a moment to steady herself, we walk together out to the hall.

By the full-length mirror, I have Mam's hairbrush, lipstick and perfume ready.

'Will you give your hair a brush?' I ask. Mam does, looking at herself in the mirror as she brushes.

'And a little bit of lippy?' I offer Mam her lipstick, which she applies with surprisingly delicate dexterity. Years of practice, I suppose, and a woman's instinct to try to always look her best. I spray a little perfume and place Mam's stylish sunhat on her crown, and we are all set to go.

We navigate the two steps out of the front door with gentle care, again no rush. I ease Mam into the front seat of the car and help her legs in as she turns to look forward. I put on her seat belt and as I step back Scamp, Mam's favourite son (all the family know who Mam's favourite is), leaps in and up onto her lap. The crew is complete. I close the door carefully and firmly.

It is a beautiful sunny afternoon on our green. The sun has moved south across the sky and is high and bright. Our stands of trees wave their leaves gently in the light summer breeze, green upon green upon green. Some neighbours call hello and wave, and small children are chased and harried by their worn-out, patient parents. The other end of the circle of life, I muse, remembering my own days as a young parent. Days when you are watching the clock, counting down the hours to when you can put the little rascals back into bed again.

We do not always drive on our afternoon out. When the weather and our energy are right, we'll take the wheelchair and go for a stroll around the Fairview and Marino area. There are many roads, greens, and circles to explore on our tour. We will often meet some of Mam's friends and neighbours as we roam.

'Hello, Pat, how are you?' Mam's friends will say with great compassion and understanding. Some will hold Mam's hand or rest a hand on her shoulder. There are tears in their eyes at times from these friends Mam has known all her life. Mam will look and smile from beneath the brim of her hat but there is no sense of recognition from her. Everybody gets the same type of response. It hurts a lot at times to witness these meetings of old friends. The sadness in me that I keep in check, but is ever-present, wells again and can make the brightest day dull into insignificance.

Some days we roll into Croydon or Marino Green. There is little traffic there and I let the dog off the lead and help Mam up out of the chair to walk a little. We stroll together, linking with one arm, and do a round, moving from sunlight to shade depending on the angle of the sun and the range of trees growing between. Our pace is slow, at times the moment almost paused.

Twelve months ago, we did not need the wheelchair. Mam was stronger on her legs, and we could walk the same streets arm in arm with the dog in tow. Some days we would do several laps of our green and the far green opposite. On these walks Mam would point at a house and tell me which family lived there. One sign of the debilitating effects of her illness was naming the people who lived in a particular house, but the names were the people who had lived there many years ago when Mam was much younger. Her recall was clear and detailed, and she told little stories about the families who once called the houses home.

Thinking about it now, I wonder if Mam had some under-standing of what was happening to her. Was she aware of her forgetfulness? Was reciting the names and stories a way of holding on to herself and keeping close to her identity?

Pushing Mam around the familiar streets at a slow and steady pace I find very calming. There is no need for us to hold a conversation. I take my time and breathe easy, trying to be totally present, relaxed and in the moment. In the moment the world goes by very slowly, and we are in our own harmony of time and movement. I have learned a lot about the fabric of my world on these simple walks. My eye takes in so much more detail. You become aware of gardens, their shape and deeper purpose and the flowering times of many different plants and trees. You notice how many types of birds are living in the world around us. You hear the hum and industry of bees in the air and notice the silence of butterflies, resplendent in their ease.

The garden city concept of yesteryear is very evident on these walks. The circle of the green means that no houses are directly facing each other, giving a privacy that's not so evident in more modern estates. There is plenty of air, sky, and nature to be had in this living experience. I point out the flowers I know to Mam, who was always a keen gardener. We pause at some and admire the colours and shapes and burst of life. Each house and garden are similar in shape and size, but also different, reflecting many things about who dwells in each one.

Mam taps on the car widow and gives me 'the look'; it's time to go for our spin. I hop in and buckle up. Five minutes' driving through the circles, greens and roads of Fairview and Marino and we are on the Howth Road and heading towards the broad sweep of glorious Dublin Bay.

Towering above the centre of the bay are arguably Dublin's most famous landmarks, the Poolbeg chimney stacks. Chimneys number 1 and 2 rise to a height of over 200 metres and are visible from most of Dublin city. Beneath the stacks the bay curves on the north side from Clontarf to Howth Head and across the bay on the south from Sandymount to Dalkey point. Within its scope it holds a world-famous wetland and bird sanctuary, many beaches and sandbanks and in its centre the mouth of the famous River Liffey and the cranes and terminals of Dublin Port.

First settled in 4000 BC and used as a staging point in the Viking invasion of Ireland in the ninth century, Dublin Bay, with its many tributary rivers, is responsible for the Dublin we know today. It is associated with the infamous Captain William Bligh of *Mutiny on the Bounty* fame, who charted the bay in the nineteenth century and was responsible for the design and construction of the refugee harbour called Kingstown, now Dún Laoghaire. Famously, James Joyce places the bay at the centre of his most famous novel, *Ulysses*, from Buck Mulligan and the Forty Foot bathing pool in Sandycove on the south side, to Leopold Bloom, Molly, and the rhododendrons on Howth Head on the north side.

Today we are driving the north arm of the bay. Out as far as Howth Head, taking in the beautiful strand of Sutton on the way. It's a journey we've made together a hundred times.

Some days we will drive the southern arm of the bay, joining the coast road as it meets Seapoint. Following that road all the way through to Monkstown and Dún Laoghaire as far as Sandycove. And on then through Bullock Harbour and the winding road as far as Sorrento Point, before heading up and over Vico Road, enjoying the seascape of Killiney, Dublin's 'Bay of Naples'.

On other days we'll turn off before Sutton on the north side and drive up through Baldoyle, touching the sea views again at Portmarnock, and on further still to the long sandy beach at Malahide and the rocky outcrops much prized by the sea swimmers of Dublin.

The July sun has reached its southern apex and floods the scene with clean and clear golden light. The sunrays glint and glide on the full tide ebbing against the coastal wall. The air is soft with the scent of brine and seaborne decay, familiar as seaside fish and chips, and as clinging.

Mam sits quiet beside me, gently rubbing faithful Scamp's ear. The fresh air and scale of the bountiful cerulean sky are, I know, beneficial to her. I have read that the colour blue forces the eyes and mind to open wider on the intake, giving an inner sense of space and calm not to be found sitting in any high-backed chair in a nursing home.

Over the past month or two there has been another change in Mam. She's taken to a gentle keening; a childhood sound mothers might make to comfort or quiet a dozing baby. The gentle sound resonates around me and within me as it must do with Mam. It's both comforting and unsettling, like a little white lie from a favourite godchild. Mam will make the sound till I interrupt her with an observation.

'There's the wooden bridge, Mam, that'll take us all the way down the pier to Dollymount.'

'Here we are at St Anne's, Mam. Can you see the ducks in the pond over the wall?'

'Will we drive down Sutton Strand and catch the view across the bay?'

It's another new thing I haven't met before. In the space around someone, and in the silence that accompanies them, you see and hear what others do not. When you have spent a lot of time up close with somebody, you do not see the obvious things any more. But a new sound, where there was quiet before, vibrates in you to the centre of your caring. Your gaze and empathy are drawn only to new things, things that might herald the next step. Your awareness is that change, however small, may be significant.

When someone new or irregular visits they are quick to pronounce the obvious like a revelation, unaware that you are way past that point, and turning in a much wider and invisible arc.

We have reached Sutton crossroads and take the right turn towards the Strand Road. As if to herald our approach, the second movement, the andante, of Rachmaninov's second piano concerto delicately falls, twirls and rises from the radio. Once past the few new modern houses, the whole of Dublin Bay opens, and the city lives below the vast, effortless sky. We turn again and roll slowly along the strand.

Mam is silent now and sits still, caressed by the music and the visual harmony of the scene unfolding before us. I stop at the white metal railing by the water's edge. We're suspended in this world, just she and I, alone. I ache that she would be well. I take her hand and am silent. Herring gulls and the smaller blackheads glide and dance on the sea breeze. Now diving and swooping towards the silver waves, then rising like the piano crescendo; now suspended and held, as if in the emotion of the music. I ache that she would be well; my silent tears make it so.

The music and the moment end, I squeeze Mam's hand and start the car again. And on we go, up through Sutton

Demesne and on to the curving Carrickbrack Road that winds around the southern flank of the hill, rising all the time. Below, Doldrum Bay and the lighthouse at Baily give names to the see-saw feelings flowing inside me. We summit at the summit and enter Thormanby Road for the descent towards the harbour views and the piers and masts nestled there below.

We find a parking space beside the eastern pier of the harbour.

'Hang on a minute, Mam, and I'll get things organised.'

I hop out into the sunlight and a nice stiff breeze. I unpack and assemble Mam's chair, cushion and blanket. I place it near her car door with the brakes on. I ease Mam out and – one, two, three – hold her hands as she stands, then turn her towards the chair and ease her down again. I place her feet on the footrests, put Scamp on his lead and we roll towards the pier walkway.

We are just approaching the walkway and Mam says, 'I want to get out and walk.'

We stop, put the brakes on, and attach Scamp's lead to the arm of the chair. One, two, three again until Mam is standing. It's an awkward manoeuvre to unbrace the chair with my foot and swing it around to one side, while linking Mam and trying not to get caught up with the dog's lead. I've had lots of practice and manage to do it. We're off again.

Fifty yards down the pier Mam wants to sit down again! We stop and do the moves in reverse so that Mam is sitting again. It's hot now, with the causeway blocking most of the sea breeze. We carry on towards the lighthouse. Another couple of minutes later Mam wants to get out of her chair again. It's turning into a circus and we're attracting attention from other strollers.

I take a deep breath and remember – patience and under-standing. It's not easy, though. I repeat the manoeuvre and twist my elbow slightly. There's a sharp stab of pain. It is the beginnings of tennis elbow; I find out weeks later when a physio tells me.

Again, we move on and again, after a few yards, Mam says, 'I want to get out and walk.'

'Ah, just sit there for a few minutes', I say, 'until we get to the bottom of the pier.'

'I want to get out and walk,' Mam says, loud enough for some passers-by to notice.

I feel their eyes on the back of my neck and imagine them saying 'You'd think he'd let his mam out to walk a little bit.'

'I want to get out and walk again' the 'poor dear' repeats, louder this time. More people look over.

'Okay then,' I say, clenching my jaw a little. I can feel my temperature rising and invisible hands pull and tear and rend my cloth of patience. Again, we manoeuvre, and the sharp pain in my elbow stabs again. We advance again a little further.

'I want to sit down in the chair,' Mam says, loud enough for people to notice.

'Will we just walk a little further? Your legs are good.' I try to encourage Mam along.

'I want to sit down again!' Louder still. I feel my under-standing slip away beneath the wheels of the chair.

'Do you want a hand to put your mam in the chair?' a kindly woman offers.

I decline, and we walk on a little. I can almost hear the lady saying, 'You'd think he'd let the woman sit down, she looks awful tired.'

I'm reddening now and it's not just from the sun's heat. I feel my patience thinning and the leering twins of disenchantment and 'why me' lurking on my shoulder.

'I want to sit down in the chair!' Mam says, louder still, petulantly.

'Okay, okay, you can sit down again,' I answer and put the brakes on. I get a dirty look from an elderly couple and a woman walking with a small child swerves away from us. It looks like a scene. My arm aches and the dog has decided to take a poop. Hysterical laughter is not far away. I put Mam in the chair again with a little less kindness than before and about-turn and head back to the car. I feel a numbness spread through my body and an 'end of transmission note' white-lining through my mind.

I relate this experience in full because it encapsulates so much of the whole caring experience. In those few moments all the elements collide and challenge. Understanding meets frustration and patience is stripped away to reveal your own deep-seated inadequacies. Hoping, wanting and wishing crash and burn against the power and relentlessness of Mam's dementia. The outwardly grown man gives way to the small boy holding his mother's hand again.

There's no one to talk to about it! There's no nodding friend saying, 'It's okay, it's different, it's as difficult for everyone.'

Mam is silent and so much in her own moment that I cannot reach her. Despair lurks in the looks around me, in the stiff breeze, in the sun's glare, and beyond, over the causeway wall and in the thousand miles of the world beyond that still.

It's here in these moments that the term 'make or break' really means something.

Does futility, and the lack of usefulness I'm feeling, gain some invisible upper hand over me?

Do I throw in the towel and say 'I can't do this any more!'?

The negative sentences begin again to crowd and taunt me: 'It's alright, everyone has a breaking point,' or 'You've done your best; let the professionals take over,' or the worst sentence of all, 'You have been a good son.'

Back in the car again, all closed in together as before, my hand grips heavily the firm roundness of the steering wheel. Perspiration rolls down my temple and the pulse and throb of the last few moments beats in tandem with my heart. I'm spiralling amidst my inner thoughts. All our lives together, our pathways, flash and turn and light across the retina of my inner eye.

Who am I anyway? Is this really happening? What is 'this'?

Make or break … make or break!

After a time, I don't know how long, a second or ten minutes, I shudder deeply through my whole frame. Like a small child on your knee trying to recover their breath after a long bout of crying for the world. I breathe out one thing and deeply inhale another. A distant voice calls to me to remember, 'You cannot do this from the outside; you must see as she sees and become one with her world.'

Again, the silver bell chimes clearly, and I see my first day of school, Mam buying me my first album, the red phone box on a London street, the welcoming open door when my entire world was falling apart. Again I shudder but know that this will be the last one.

The wave has found, turned, and washed over me. I commit now, with no fear of the future or what it may bring, that

I will never leave Mam, and I will see this through, on our terms, whatever it takes from us or whatever it gives to us.

I feel a turning again. A full turning into our situation. I lock on to the true reality of what's happening here and now to Mam an' me. I strike our flag deep into the bedrock of the love we have between us. I've come through the crucible and find that the fire and smoke and crash have burned away all my doubts and fears.

'We'll be alright,' I say aloud and turn to Mam.

Our eyes smile together as one, our walk down the pier forgotten.

'Will we go home and have a little dinner, love?' I ask.

'I'd like that,' she kindly replies.

8.

Tony

It is Tuesday 10 July 2018. I am standing in the lobby of the Radisson Blu hotel in Letterkenny, looking out through the floor-to-ceiling windows. The morning sky is lightly overcast, as it often is in Donegal, the most north-westerly county in Ireland. In the hotel forecourt, over a hundred people are wearing, donning, or passing out blue T-shirts. Printed on the T-shirts is a map of Ireland with a yellow balloon on a yellow string and the words 'Walk While You Can' written across it. The lobby around me is full of people, old and young, and all are wearing the same blue T-shirts.

Outside I see Michael Murphy, the captain of the Donegal football team, chatting with someone. He's wearing one. The mayor of Letterkenny, Ian McGarvey, is there too, proudly displaying his golden chain of office. I can see faces I recognise from Ballymun, Mount Merrion and UCD. Tony's best friend Declan is also there, smiling and chatting with three ladies who are wearing yellow hi-vis vests over their T-shirts. There are yellow balloons floating in the air and a man has a blue cardboard sign under his arm that says, 'Walk with Tony.' There's great energy and animation in the scene and laughter and chatting in the air. No one is paying any attention to the sky above.

In a corner of the lobby behind me, Mam sits in her navy cardigan and slacks, talking with her three blond, handsome grandsons, Rian, Oscar and Michael. Their mam and dad too are dressed in blue, looking fit and ready for the day's exercise ahead. Through the throng my brother Tony appears in his electric wheelchair, wearing black shorts and the blue T-shirt. Michelle steps forward to open the door for him, and as he wheels outside a great cheer and applause fill the air. It is the first day of the walk to Ballydehob in Cork, over 350 miles away as the crow flies. A walk that will take the participants the best part of four weeks to complete and will hopefully raise much-needed funding and awareness for sufferers of motor neurone disease.

'Come on, Mam, will we go outside and join the fun?'

'Why is everyone wearing blue T-shirts?', she asks, standing up and linking my arm.

'It's for Tony's charity walk, Mam', I remind her, 'to raise money for motor neurone research and support.'

'Motor neurone? What's that?'

'It is a bad illness, Mam, that hurts people. Come on out outside, they're taking a group photo.'

Everyone was gathering for the photo for the next day's copy of the *Donegal Daily*. There was a camera crew too, making a documentary about Tony and his WWYC campaign.

'Come on in here, Mam,' says a smiling Tony, and Mam takes her place behind his right shoulder. Poignantly to me, Mam places her hand on Tony's shoulder in that familiar gesture I saw in other photos of Mam with her sisters. It catches my breath as I step aside. Mam looks delighted, with her crown of silver hair and her other hand raised. Her smile, as always, beams, eyes bright and cheeks raised, a smile of genuine happiness.

And then they were off. Tony, in his purpose-built green mountain trike wheelchair, is pushed by Pat, our youngest, and flanked by his nephews, friends and colleagues. He waves to the good people of Letterkenny, smiling broadly all the way. Ahead is the first stage of the journey, a 19 km hike to Baly-bofey, across the River Swilly and the rolling hills of Donegal. It's so like Tony, despite his illness, to be leading from the front, always a doer, an organiser of things and people, always a leader.

My first memory of him was much the same, although I was only five or six and he was five years older. We were in our upstairs bedroom in Fairview Green. Tony was saying Mass, or trying to. I was an altar boy and Tony was giving out communion, or a piece of bread torn from a batch loaf, as I knelt in front of him. That's all I recall of the 'Mass', because immediately afterwards I ran down the stairs and out onto the green to play soccer with my friends. Not Tony, though. He came out five minutes later in his black referee's uniform, the only ref's outfit for twenty miles around, outside the national GAA stadium of Croke Park down the road. He also had a whistle and a notebook. He organised us into teams and away we went, him blowing his whistle and cajoling and enjoying the game in his way as much as the rest of us.

When we moved to Santry and our bigger house, Tony organised quizzes in the garage beside our kitchen. He, of course, was the quiz master and wrote out all the questions and kept the score. He was so far ahead of us even then. Our bedrooms were connected on the left upper side of the house. When one day I discovered my model airplanes mysteriously smashed to pieces he was a shoulder to cry on. 'We'll get you some new ones, Kieran. If you stop crying, we can have a go at fixing them up again.' We did, to no real avail, but I remember that moment well, even though it's 45 years ago. I think we all remember a kindness when we are feeling very low. Kindness was a quality Tony had, and showed, from an early age. A quality that many people, in many ways, would experience and take comfort and strength from in Tony's company.

When our parents separated and we moved home a few doors down the road, Tony was the one carrying the furniture with Mam. One evening, when my father came home early from work, they were carrying a bookcase down the road to the new house. On spotting his car they both had to jump over a neighbour's low wall and hide in the garden.

As we all tried to adjust to life without our father, things at home became slightly chaotic. My brother and I started to hang around with the 'wrong crowd' and there was friction bubbling beneath the surface at home. Tony was ever the peacemaker and stood firmly by Mam's side, intervening when he could. He very kindly offered me some money one day if I would stop 'heading up the road' and start to play with my gentler friends again. I refused and regret my decision even today.

Some years later, when we moved to the parish of Iona in Glasnevin, Tony and I shared a bedroom. Tony at that stage was firmly on the path to priesthood. He was working too, and we did not see that much of each other anymore.

Sitting now with pen and paper, the next years of our family pass by like scenery through the windows of a moving train. Boarding that train on a cold and wet misty morning, the world around all black, white, and clouds of grey steam and smoke. It could be Holyhead, back in 1986 when I first took the boat and a train to London. Like, as yesterday, I see the green canvas rucksack, containing all I possessed, over one shoulder and my denim jacket buttoned up to the collar.

As our train pulls out of the station, a faint image reflected in the half fogged-up carriage window, is a morning scene from our kitchen in Glasnevin. The Superser gas fire is lit and hums away just below the level of the radio. Mam, in her soft pink dressing gown and slippers, stands over the cooker tending to some bacon frying. I sit with David at the table, we are dressed for travelling, ready to depart. Pat has his full school uniform on and stands watching. Tony pours from a pot of tea into mugs spread on our blue and white Formica table.

It's like an allegory of an Irish family. Eldest brother departs to the priesthood, the next emigrates as far away as possible, Australia in our case. Like a punishment for the way things turned out or a relief from where they might have gone. The next son is for across the water, not far enough to be really gone, close enough to always be a worry. And the youngest, held by the promise of 'finishing your education', becomes the eldest by default and by standing still in the kitchen.

The steam rising from the mugs blends with the fogged-up windows, and the train pulls out into the early morning's faintest glimmer of a sunrise. Gathering momentum, the station slips and falls behind. We begin to roll in-country and beneath rising hills a granite country house, east-facing in the faint silver light, grows to Clonliffe College. We walk up the long driveway to deposit Tony in its seminary. Tony is so fresh-faced and innocent-looking amongst the lofty ceilings, stern portraits and parquet floors. Mam looks so happy, balancing a cup and saucer, and the conversation with the other hopefuls' mams. Pat and I slip away and find a snooker table and the Pope's chair in a downstairs room for our entertainment. We're discovered and leave chastised and 'selfish'. Behind the closing wooden door Tony was gone, into the dark recesses and many chambers of that monolithic place.

As our carriage sways gently from side to side, dream-like, the four seats and table opposite become occupied and alive with every aunt and uncle from Mam's side. Frank and Nancy, Tim and Kathleen, Roseleen, John, Pauline, and Betty and Jimmy. There is lots of laughter and more tea and cakes; familiar kitchens and sitting together on coloured sofas in front rooms. There is playing in gardens with our many happy cousins and twenty-firsts with the ham and salad buffets. Singing too, Mam's sweet voice carrying the melody. Interwoven and watching, they are a constant benevolent and comforting presence during the years ahead and around us. They are here for the remainder of this journey. Though along the way, in slow ones, they will all alight permanently.

We cross another bridge now and, looking down into the grey river beneath our spinning wheels, I see the faint shimmering outline of the towers and spars of London town. Hovering too, my young face and that of my girlfriend looking back at us. So full of early beginnings, like parenthood and responsibility. Barely butterflies we were, in those formative and frightening days, too young, though, to be afraid. There was colour and real magic in the early moments as we fought for us against the world.

And a baby's cries, heralding the first of our family's next generation. The scale of the city, the anonymity, the lack of care all became a distance. The distance between everything became a distance between us. Afterwards, and home again, we tumbled from one place to the next for many years, before finally breaking apart. I stand again in the darkness, hand resting on the Formica.

Again, the train's momentum pushes us forward. We are gliding now. Around and above us green fields roll in opposites and a sky of clearest infinity watches through the glass skylights. Mam sits opposite me now and we are holding hands across the table. 'I know, Mam, what you mean to me, what you have done for me and my girls.' She holds my hand tightly. Through our fingertips I see her walk to Mass each morning to pray or sing or both. Her friends and neighbours walk beside and around her. In that clear daylight, I see the packed church for Tony's ordination. Him prostrate in crucifix, at the bishop's feet, and now raised and called, for the first time, Father. And the joy of Mam, so personal and so deserved. Her joy is for Tony, and his chance and opportunity to be free, to follow his dreams. As I watch she breaths lightly on her curled fingers and shines them on her shoulder, her show of pride at her son's moment of glory. We share tears together, both of us knowing what is to come.

There is a tunnel now and we plunge into its darkness and noise. The train's roar and tunnel form envelop us, and everything inside is refracted and reflected. The skylight's opaque into overhead lockers and we are flying now inside a jumbo jet at 50,000 feet on our first, or fourth, or last, long journey to the furthest place west; to catch up with our émigré in the outback of Australia. Here is sunlight, searingly bright and unforgiving, stretching across a prehistoric and largely unaffected landscape. Flocks of colourful, chattering parrots astound our European eyes with their commonality. From an old gum tree, a kookaburra, a king of fishers, laughs childishly, as we laugh at kangaroos and koalas curled and soft in our daughters' arms. The family has grown as we swelter beneath a Christmas tree and the nieces and nephews frolic in the bright blue swimming pool, such a long, long way, thankfully, from the early morning of our yesteryear.

I have dozed in my seat under the spell and rhythm of remembrance. I slip from my body, and ghost above my sleeping self. My head rests on my soft shoulder and in my left hand, outstretched and resting lightly on the table, I hold a photograph. It is a perfect picture of symmetry and harmony. Mam stands centre, in wedding mauve, floral headpiece and signature smile. She is flanked by her four tall sons, wearing the white roses of the bridal party, arms across each other's shoulders, encompassing the reason we are all alive and here together on the day. And our Pat, the youngest and the groom, beaming brightest, his face reflecting his three blond sons and his love for his wife, Michelle. Above, the faint blue Kilternan sky, laced with wisps of high-flying cirrus, frames us and the blue church of Our Lady of the Wayside, forever to be remembered as one of the happiest days of our lives.

I stand at the half-opened window of the carriage doorway smoking a cigarette, smoking as I have done through all the days of my life. Through the exhale the countryside flashes by and the rolling hills give way to an open plain, boundless, and touching to the sky. In the near distance longhorns are chaperoned by Stetson-wearing men on horses, and at their feet blue bonnets leave a trail to the old Alamo.

It is country I have visited before, seeking a paradox, a father who is not a father. In his last moments we came when we did not have to, a measure of our rearing, a rearing he had chosen not to be a part of. Only an echo remained, and we saw, through the tired frame, ourselves, the only worthwhile melody from a lonely soul banging his own drum. But still, for many years after, a sadness lingered in me for what might have been. An echo too of the dark paths my life had taken but also others that I might have taken. We disassembled all he had and made and remade it for our days ahead. And for our dear Mam, finally a widow, finally free to join the secretary of her past.

Evening has come silently on; the carriage lamps are reflected and sway as strings of pearls or Christmas lights in the darkened glass and framed rectangular windows.

Christmas.

If a word can capture the hills and valleys journeyed in a lifetime, it is this. Presents or presence. Who is here, who has gone before, empty chairs and places set. Laughter from the other room as you scrape the plates alone, with faltering or aching heart and silent tears accompanying your thousand-yard stare.

Walking through our family carriage, each table is like a Christmas of yesteryear. A train set with a figure-eight track and cowboys and Indians spread out on the front room carpet; and matching knitted jumpers from Betty. In the days when families called to each other, and the year our father was gone, my aunts and uncles in suits and flowers arrived; and a can of stout or Smithwick's brought out from under the stairs along with their laughter and loving affection.

And Iona, pulling crackers and wearing paper hats, us all together, with the fire blazing and John Lennon's 'Imagine' playing in the air and smoke around us. In the chaplain's house in UCD, Tony hosting, bountiful on the elongated table with our biggest smiles all around. Ballinteer with our in-laws Anne and Larry and our spreading family numbering over a score. Opening the presents together after lunch, like the cast of some American TV show, unwrapping and joking. It all seems so like yesterday.

And the final table, the last Christmas, our own family's Spiritus Mundi, laid long in the white and light of the Mount Merrion kitchen. Our wine glasses catching the candlelight as it reflects in the large photograph hanging on the wall, a picture Tony took of Gethsemane. We are all there in the reflection, placed amongst the garden and its lake. Like shadows, that with troubled sight know the future.

Tony has slipped in his stockinged feet, and we struggle to right him into a kitchen chair. He explained he had fallen during the week after his knee gave way and his elbow was troubling him too. We were all concerned, but not overly so. Mam's illness was manifesting increasingly, and our focus was in her direction. Like Tony, he played it down and minimised it, and promised to call his doctor after the Christmas break. We cajoled him as brothers do and Mam kissed him and held him tight as mothers do.

And now I hear Yeats, and the power of his words, though written a century earlier, strike me deep and with supreme force:

Somewhere in sands of the desert
A shape with lion body …
A gaze blank and pitiless …
Is moving its slow thighs …

A few weeks later I rang Tony.

'The doctor said I might have had a mild stroke. At least it's not motor neurone disease,' he said.

The significance of Tony mentioning MND was that our cousin Seamus had passed recently due to complications from contracting MND. He was the first in our wider family to have this terrible illness, but tragically not to be the last.

But the doctor was wrong.

In a text message to everyone a few weeks later, Tony explained that he had been diagnosed with MND.

Our entire world lurched, and in that movement all the glass and crockery slid from our table for ever, and crashed and broke around us. All reflections are gone. There is to be no more when confronted with this kind of reality.

Again Yeats,

... while all about it
Reel shadows of the indignant desert birds.
The darkness drops again ...
And what rough beast, its hour come round at last
Slouches towards Bethlehem to be born?

Again, I stand in the darkness, this silent movie playing for my singular audience. I am alone, as we all are, when confronted by our own actions and reactions. I feel the numbness again from my head to the soles of my feet. The record's turning but the needle has been raised. Mam sits as my silent witness behind a pane of glass, behind my pain. I see Gethsemane again and a battle to accept, a battle to understand. The agony of why, the fear of 'why me?'.

Our train has stopped too. I alight in the small hills of west Cork, wearing the blue of the Walk While You Can campaign, and with my brothers we push our Tony, in his green mountain trike chair, those final miles into the crowd and cheer of Ballydehob.

Tony's campaign to raise funds and awareness in the fight against MND has been a resounding success on all fronts. He has galvanised the country with the power of his actions and personality. He has succeeded in bringing the plight of all MND sufferers to our collective consciousness, ensuring that it will remain there in the years ahead.

But the walk and the effort have taken their toll on him, as he was told it would before he started. Selfless as always, he went ahead anyway, pushing his future out of the way for the greater good. Now, back in his home again, things have altered around him. His house has been converted to help him, and those with him, cope and assist with the debilitating effects of his illness. The reality of his situation becomes ever present and ominous.

Again, Tony shows his mettle and decides to write his own story. With the help of his primary caregiver, Adam, they manage to produce a beautiful book about his life and the wisdom he has found living it. *Live While You Can*, he called it.

It is a testament that we, his family, take great comfort and succour from in his absence. Mam looks at it now every day, its blue cover never far from her line of sight.

And now it is August 2019. Wednesday the 28th in the parish house of Mount Merrion, Tony's home for the last ten years. A home in a parish we have all become comfortable and familiar with. A gathering place, as it is today and has been for the last few days. Tony has taken the final turn on the pathway of his illness.

Now, as evening has come on, and sunlight streams through his blinded window, we have gathered, his nearest and dearest, to say goodbye, for now. He fought the good fight and assured himself a place among the angels.

In the air around us, the shades of family hover closely with welcoming arms, for a son, a brother and a father coming home.

We wish it to be so.

Late Fragment
And did you get what
you wanted from this life, even so?
I did.
And what did you want?
To call myself beloved, to feel myself
beloved on the earth.

Raymond Carver

9.

DINNER

We are back home, parked in our driveway, after a slow and uneventful drive back down the coast. Mam's silence has deepened, as if she herself got a little fright earlier. I take her hand gently and feel her aged fingers and the warmth within. My touch brings her slowly round, and she exhales a long, shallow breath, which makes my heart ache again.

'Did you enjoy the drive, Mam?' I whisper, to the silence that is holding her.

I see in her blue-green eyes her presence coming to the surface, and as it breaks her smile crests too. 'I did,' she replies simply. 'Will we go inside now?'

It's my turn to exhale and I rouse myself towards the next part of our day.

Inside again, I hang up Mam's coat and before I begin the prep for dinner, take the opportunity to put her in the stairlift for a toilet check upstairs. The chair is an absolute necessity these days. It whirrs and ascends slowly with Mam holding on for dear life, like she's on a rollercoaster. I've told her a hundred times that it is safe, but I suppose she forgets, and each time is like her first.

I go before her up the stairs and use the chairs remote control to manoeuvre her up and around the bend. The chair beeps and turns at the top and faces Mam towards the upstairs landing. I unbuckle Mam's seatbelt and raise the footrests.

'Okay, Mam, let's stand up.' I take her outstretched hands.

'One, two, three, and stand.' I lean back and raise her gently to standing and then we walk to the bathroom and the task ahead. This bathroom routine never quite feels right to me. Yet the familiarity of the routine adds to the closeness we have together. In these moments, our paths weave and turn together. I am helping Mam but benefiting from being able to do so. Each action helps to pay back a little of the kindness Mam has shown in raising and caring for me. I feel deep inside me this balance is being counted and stored towards the final eventuality of Mam's illness.

Some minutes later, Mam changed and fresh, hands washed, towel straightened, we hold hands again and move back to the awaiting chair. Mam sits and smiles and we buckle up for the descent.

There is an hour before dinner, and I make Mam a nice cuppa with a plain biscuit. Chocolate ones are out now. They don't help her body and she doesn't seem to miss them. Mam sits at ease in her big armchair, the trusty Scamp sitting snugly beside her. The TV is showing one of her favourites, *Sherlock Holmes*. The black and white version with Basil Rathbone as Holmes and Nigel Bruce as his trusty sidekick Doctor Watson. Mam never tires of watching the re-runs of these classics.

'He is the best Sherlock Holmes out of them all!' she would say, and I agree.

The archetype of the fog of London and the deep mists of the English moors. *The Hound of the Baskervilles*, *The Voice of Terror* and *The Scarlet Claw* are among her favourites. They were all made at the height of the Second World War but they stand the test of time, and compete against the many remakes very well. Mam watches with great concentration and works her way through the tea and biscuit. My youngest girl, Eve, who has a great kinship with her granny, has appeared, and sits with her watching *Sherlock*, a kindred spirit and convert to Conan Doyle's hero.

A large part of each day's routine is organised around mealtimes. Our body clock works independently from the mind, and it is a tangible anchor that a person can hold on to. Nourishing Mam's body is something I can and do have an influence over.

Just about all Mam's evening meals are home cooked, usually by me. Although I have worked in the catering industry all my life, my experience and expertise have mostly been on the other side of the hotplate, front of house. In my early twenties, as part of my management training for Trust House Forte Hotels in London, I worked for six months in a hotel kitchen.

I worked at the Cavendish Hotel on Jermyn Street, a posh four-star located off Piccadilly. The quality of the guests reflected its location, as did the quality of the management and staff working there. The kitchen was no exception. A full team of experienced professionals was led by the veteran and charismatic Spanish head chef Mr Jack Rivas. The kitchen was organised into sections, with commis chefs, chefs de partie and a tough cadre of sous-chefs. I took my turn in the vegetable section, peeling and turning huge bags of veg for hours, then a stint with the cold starters, sandwiches and salads. Finally, a turn in the fierce heat and pressure of the sauce and main course section. Despite the different chefs' best efforts at training me, I never really got the hang of it.

I did get to see the catering world from the other side, though, and this experience has always stayed with me. Proper preparation, portion control and timing are all skills that I became aware of and developed, skills I use now in organising meals for the family. Chef Rivas would be proud, I am sure.

Thirty minutes later, the kitchen scene is reflected along the edge of the chopping knife I am holding. Steam rises, sucked up and towards the extractor from the metal pots bubbling away on the packed stove, and the air above the brimming pans shimmers with latent heat. On the long chopping board in front of me, the ingredients for Mam's salad glisten. The back door is open wide to the garden, and the sound of my neighbour mowing his lawn floats in to join the mouthwatering aroma of frying garlic and chorizo in the air.

It's a full house this evening at Casa Coote and my meagre cheffing talents are under pressure. I've a vegetarian to contend with; two middle ones who will eat anything, as long as they don't have to make it themselves; and the eldest, slightly spoilt by her once juvenile parents, picks and chooses and de-selects as she sees fit. And then there's Mam, who has her own menu, for as long as she is able to. Finally, the chef, organised and overheating, with appetite long gone, is in 'just getting this service over' mode.

There are plenty of offers of help from the girls, but the kitchen, at eight feet by five at best, does not allow any. All available counter space is in use and there is only a narrow walkway down the centre. As it is I must step out into the back garden to allow the eldest daughter room to step in and fill the obligatory water glasses.

Outside I hear Leonard Cohen on the radio saying 'So Long …' to Marianne. A memory flows back to me of Paros, Greece, and the starlight of the first evening I ever heard it, more than thirty years ago now. From the sultry outside terrace of the flat-roofed one-storey house, the song followed us down to the silver half-arc of the sandy beach of Dolphin Bay. And on, into the black water, as we dived and swam under the bright moonlight. Then, standing waist deep and hurling handfuls of luminosity into the night sky, we watched wide-eyed as the mineral content of the water glittered like stardust in the sky around us. Like Leonard, we too, forgot to pray and laughed and cried and laughed again.

'Are you alright, Dad?' the eldest asks, pulling me softly from the still warm sand of my memory.

'Yes, thank you, dear, all is well.'

It is time to put a shape on this meal and I'm all action for the next fifteen minutes. Mam can feed herself still, requiring a little encouragement along the way. A visually appetising plate of food can help too. I have prepared a selection of cold meat, cheese and salad, each element cut into bite-size pieces. It's simple enough fare and I've brought all my artistic qualities into arranging it to look as tempting as possible. There is a nice mug of tea too and some lightly buttered brown bread on the side.

I'm pleased with myself as I put the plate down on the little folding table in front of Mam. She's in her big armchair with a couple of cushions propping her forward.

'The tea is hot, love, blow on it first before you take a sip.'

The girls and I are ranged along the couch and extra chair, TV-dinner style, munching the various combinations of pasta plus and garlic bread. On the TV the US true crime show *48 Hours* is playing. In a scene from an interview room a detective grills a potential perp. In response to the perp's explanation the detective shouts at him, 'That's a load of crap you're giving me!'

And quick as you like, Mam leans back in her cushioned chair and with her left foot pushes the table away from her and says loudly, 'Speaking of crap, look what they've given me for my dinner tonight!'

We all freeze in amazement and disbelief. All eyes turn to Mam, then to me, and in unison we all burst out laughing. It's the best laugh we have shared together in what seems like an awfully long time. The look on Mam's face is priceless. The poor dear gets a bit of a fright, and then, as if what she said has just dawned on her, her beautiful smile breaks out, followed by the music of her laughter.

Outside in the back garden after dinner, the sun hiding behind the red-ridged terracotta rooftops, I think about the incident. Has it upset me somehow, bruised my ego maybe? What is going on with Mam? How strangely and unpredictably this dementia, or is Alzheimer's, affects Mam's thoughts and actions. Did she mean what she said earlier? It sounded so convincing. And yet afterwards she happily ate all her dinner, the moment completely forgotten.

It is all so unsettling at times. It is beyond the level of my mind to fully comprehend. I try to go deeper into the moment, to find something that makes some sense to me. I close my eyes and follow a breath down as it fills my lungs and raises my chest. The smell of the freshly cut grass follows me to the centre. It stirs a memory from my shared past with Mam. The memory is from here in the back garden, the open side, with the ivied and grey block wall. It is from the summer of 1974. Our neighbour Dinny, the local handyman from the far green, adds wet cement to trowel and lays it along the top of the next row. The new wall he is building is to replace the old iron railings that have always marked the boundary and divide between the back lane and the house next door. It's part of the shutting in, shutting out, that starts to happen when we become afraid of things.

There's a towel or blanket spread on the grass and I sit on it watching Dinny at his work. He is three blocks high and already our view of the world is changing. I can smell the grass and hear Mam singing in the kitchen behind me. A passing cloud shuts out the sun and the shadow sends a chill that makes me rise from the blanket. Dinny has stopped too and wipes his brow as he checks for rain. From over and beyond the new wall a wood pigeon starts her call, and to my little ears it sounds like

'Your fear means nothing,
your fear means nothing,
your fear means nothing.'

And then Mam alights from the kitchen with twirling skirt, and a thick-cut sandwich and a mug of tea for Dinny. She scoops me up and folds me in to her, and the cloud moves on, and the sun comes out again.

I exhale deeply and blink in my mind's eye, awake again to the present moment. I have reached in and found an answer that makes sense to me.

Truly we all hold the answers to everything we need inside us. We are all made from the same thing, stardust most likely.

And ancient wisdom held in the air we breathe, breathed before by somebody, possibly wondering aloud too, what is it all about and what is it that makes us so afraid.

The world seems right again, for now.

No need to shut anything in, no need to shut anything out.

10.

AT THE END OF THE DAY

Mam continued to work part-time as she moved into her sixties and beyond. She was now helping the nuns in High Park convent and nursing home, in the mornings and sometimes in the afternoons too. There was another very special reason that Mam was working there. Her sister Pauline was a long-term Alzheimer's patient in the nursing home. Pauline had worked in High Park for many years before the onset of her illness. Thankfully, a place was found for her there amongst long-time friends and colleagues.

Its location allowed regular visits from Mam and the rest of the family. I visited with Mam many times, being her part-time chauffeur. It was always a difficult visit seeing Pauline's decline, both physically and mentally. Equally difficult was watching the wearing effect it had on Mam. They were the best of friends and had hoped to spend their later years together.

Witnessing both sides of this illness – the patient, and the carer – has always stayed with me. Mam's selfless commitment, the love in evidence always and her ability to see through the illness to the person beneath are things I learnt from her. Pauline's inability to do anything about her illness, her dependence on others, and her hope that somebody really cared for her were all things I saw first-hand over the years. I learnt from her too.

It has been twenty years since. Now each day I replay and repay the things I have learnt. How little Mam and I knew of the shape the paths our lives would take. The rise and fall of our momentum, the twin beating of our hearts, the sharing of sunrise and sunsets. Fate must have placed a hand on our destiny, swirling our worlds and making everything turn out like it needed to.

Another consequence of Mam working in High Park was her decision to learn to drive for the first time. No one knew where this idea came from, but Mam, in her quiet way, was determined to do it. I believe she was fed up with walking up and down the hill of Gracepark Road. Also, Mam was regularly attending to her choral duties with the choir in Iona. Her dear friends John and Rina would be there to give her a lift. John was a busy man and, would admit himself, not as punctual as our Mam liked. Mam never liked to be late and was always early wherever she went.

Sure enough, Mam embarked on a series of driving lessons and bought herself a little Fiesta and some L plates. Before long she was driving on her own up and down to Iona and Gracepark. Illegally of course, as a learner, but we had not the heart to tell her. Mam had not committed a crime since the day when, as a young girl, she stole an apple from a shop. Her Mam found out and marched her around to the storekeeper to apologise and give back the part of the apple she had not eaten. Her lesson learned, she never offended again. Until now of course!

Mam's modus operandi when starting off in the car was to quickly accelerate out of her parking space and shoot off down the road. Other cars' wing mirrors might be bumped on the way, and local cats and dogs learned to move fast at the sound of her approaching engine. It was a sight to behold and a hair-raising experience if you happened to be a passenger with her.

'It's the starting off and the stopping I don't like', she often said, 'the rest of it I find easy enough.'

Mam's career as a burgeoning race driver ended after her first driving test. Gina and I drove her up to the test centre in Raheny. Mam was incredibly nervous and recited a novena under her breath all the way. Mam was wearing a lovely hand-knitted wool jumper and a long matching pleated skirt, very much the grandmother. She went into the office to register and came out a moment later with the driving instructor clutching his clipboard. He was about the same age and height as Mam and had a beard, glasses, waistcoat, and wore a flat cap. They looked like an old married couple together. We had left the car parked advantageously for Mam to start and gave her a thumbs up and a smile as she got into her little blue car.

True to form, Mam shot off and went around the first corner very fast, almost on two wheels. We could hear the instructor squealing 'Mrs Coote!' as they disappeared around the corner.

Fifteen minutes later they arrived back and jerked to a stop about 3 feet from the curb. The instructor clambered out of the car a little paler than when he had entered. We waved again at Mam as she followed him into the test centre. Mam reappeared a minute later holding her long test sheet, which looked well marked, and had a couple of holes in it.

'How'd you get on?' I asked when she got back into the car.

'I failed', she said. 'That little baldy oul fella was terrified.'

'Ah! That is a pity. It can make you nervous when they start marking the test sheet each time you make a little mistake', I said, trying to comfort her.

'Well, he never stopped writing from the moment we started,' she said. 'But I think it was the going through the red light so fast that really done it for me!'

Evening has come on; darkness gathers silently in the corners of the room, and the clock shows ten. The girls have dispersed upstairs or are gone out and about. Mam yawns and I catch her eye.

'Are you ready for bed Mam?' I ask.

'I'll just catch the headlines first', she says, as the music begins for RTE News.

That's my cue to prepare everything for Mam's bedtime. It seems an age since this morning and Puccini, as I tread the thirteen steps upstairs again. It has been a full day and now there is one last task for the day to be completed.

Mam's bedroom window faces west and in the sky above the high hedges and rooftops the last of the day's light cele-brates in orange and palest gold. I turn down Mam's blanket and puff up her pillows. Mams pyjamas and nightwear are in her tall dresser, her creams in the bedside locker. I arrange things, moving her change of clothes to the bathroom. Here the towel is lined up and Mam's toothbrush is made ready. The small important details only take a practiced moment.

Back downstairs, Mam is in a study watching the world news. It all sounds bad as usual, and I ignore it.

'Are you ready for bed Mam?' I ask again. It is like this morning, waiting for Mam's attention to turn to me, for her to be in the moment. It takes a minute but at the third time of asking, she looks toward me and nods. I lower the volume down completely and step in front of Mam, blocking her view of the tv, offering her my hands to take.

She does and smiles sweetly, eyes wide and charming.

I brace my legs.

'And 1, 2, 3, lift', I say, leaning back gently, and Mam rises slowly, legs creaking. The poor dear is quite frail and light.

'Now we will hold for a second, get your bearings Love, and move forward when you are ready.'

After a moment she's ready and we shuffle around and out the door into the hall and nicely pirouette into the awaiting stair chair. Seat belt on, footrest down.

'Here we go again Mam.' Mam whirrs up and away, holding on tightly. At the top of the stairs, we unbuckle and again 1, 2, 3, lift, and proceed with the bathroom routine. A few minutes later, routine complete, Mam clean and fresh, I lead her back to her bedroom, and she plonks down happily onto her bed.

The tiredness from the day has gathered in the soft lines under her eyes.

'Did you have a good day today, Mam?' I ask, kneeling in front of her, holding her hands and looking into her eyes.

Mam comes to the surface and is present in this moment. It is a question we have been sharing together at the end of each day for the last few months. Like a reckoning of the day and what it held for us. And below that, on a deeper level, a soul-to-soul enquiry along the inner channel of our lifelong, personal, and unspoken, relationship.

'I did have a good day', she replies with emphasis. I know she means it and she grips my hands a little tighter.

'I did too Love, I enjoyed spending our day together.'

I turn up the volume a little on Mam's radio. Lyric again, and the opening notes of the 'Adagio of Spartacus and Phrygia'.

I help lift Mam's legs into the bed and she turns slowly and slides down onto her side, her lovely face framed against the linen white pillow. Her eyes close slowly, almost immediately. I cross to the window and draw the curtains together, closing out the last of the light and the day gone by. I tuck Mam in with her light coverlet and switch off her bedside lamp. The landing light is still on, and the bedroom remains full of silhouette.

For a moment I stand over Mam's resting frame and feel a surge of love filling my heart. I see my shadowed reflection in the mirror that hangs above the fireplace. It has been a full day; it has been a good day. From *La bohème* in the early morning and the first cup of tea, through to the nourishing and washing of late morning. We've had second breakfast and a long drive out the north Dublin coast. We walked and talked and listened to some fine music. Enjoyed the fresh sea air and blue sky and summer's heat in between and around us.

Then home again to family dinner and laughter. Familiar and comforting sounds. And now at the end of the day, as the light of the world fades towards nighttime, we are safe and together. It is as it has always been, as parent and child. How we made it through the day is not important now at this moment. Just this moment remains, and it can be anything we want it to be. It is what I want it to be.

And for Mam, her beginnings are here in this room. Through the forties and early trials and tribulations of school days, to her happier days as a legal secretary. Marrying a soldier, who did not remain one. Having five sons and all that entails, including the death of a baby. Through the hiatus and total separation, to redemption and the choirs and good people of Iona. Then returning home, safe at last and forever. And in between her grandchildren and travelling all over the world. And finally, tonight, as has been the case for many nights since, asleep in her own bed in her own room where it all began over eighty years earlier. It is what she would want it to be.

And I, on this day alone, have journeyed inward to the deepest places of my heart and soul. I have witnessed all the true colors of emotion reflected in my inner pool of conscious-ness. I have felt the drops and heard the quiet echo of my hopes and dreams. I have had visions of the past and the future in vivid light and shade. I have remembered all the days of my life, with and without my mother. Again, I see my shadowed reflection in the mirror, from boyhood through to man. From son to father to son again. I stand clear and true in the light of the choices and decisions I have made.

Again, a silver trumpet calls from far away in the distance. Once more my inner eye catches sight of the rolling grassy hills of some kind of heaven. There, standing proud, I see the shades of my two brothers who have gone before. And below, arranged around a picnic spread on the lawn, my aunties and uncles animated in their expectation.

'Goodnight, Mam', I whisper, 'I'll see you in the morning.'